A Chronicle of CIVIL WAR HAMPTON, VIRGINIA

A Chronicle of CIVIL WAR HAMPTON, VIRGINIA

Struggle and Rebirth on the Homefront

ALICE MATTHEWS ERICKSON

Foreword by Wythe Holt

Published by The History Press
Charleston, SC 29403
www.historypress.net

First published 2014

Manufactured in the United States

ISBN 978.1.62619.225.6

Library of Congress CIP data applied for.

Notice: The information in this book is true and complete to the best of our knowledge. It is offered without guarantee on the part of the author or The History Press. The author and The History Press disclaim all liability in connection with the use of this book.

Contents

Foreword

When I was a child, I loved to listen to the stories my grandfathers told me. Like most of us, they had led interesting and varied lives, but perhaps unlike many folks today, their stories—some of which had been passed down to them by their own parents and grandparents—chiefly concerned relations among large numbers of cousins and friends within what today seems a relatively small geographic area, the Lower Virginia Peninsula. They spoke of a slower-moving time when the Peninsula was small town and agrarian, when many people made their livings from seafood harvesting, when Hampton, Phoebus, Fox Hill, Newport News, Hilton Village, Aberdeen, Warwick, Poquoson, Grafton and Yorktown (to say nothing of Fort Monroe, Langley Field and Fort Eustis) seemed to be distant from and almost alien to one another in terms of miles and in terms of habits, suspicions and allegiances. Most of the stories were centered (and sometimes even touched) on a huge elephant in the room: the Southern loss in the Civil War and its aftermath.

Viewed collectively today, their tales formed an important part of the history of a very different time, scarred by Jim Crow segregation, with large, close-knit families living and visiting and feuding with one another while they and their interwoven communities struggled to deal with and emerge from the politically, economically and emotionally devastating occurrences of the four-year struggle that sundered the nation, killed or maimed hundreds of thousands, tore up the Peninsula and set free an entire enslaved black race. Cousins, carpetbaggers and complicated, often harsh and explosive relationships of race and gender filled their stories, which I have longed to find time to write down.

Fortunately for all of us, my former across-the-street neighbor Alice Matthews Erickson has done justice to such a vision, writing the history of Hampton during and after the Civil War through the lens of stories from the Hickman family, mostly those she remembered having been told when, as a child herself, she was fortunate to have stayed with her own sturdy, storytelling granny (Angelina Hickman Parramore). Like several of my forebears and many other locals, most of the Hickmans left home and lived in North Carolina during the war, returning home afterward. Unlike many, they had a working farm to return to, since the men of the family resolutely braved military occupation to remain on their land, a large farm off what are now called Woodland and Fox Hill Roads at the headwaters of Hampton Creek. Old-time Hamptonians may recall the Charles Windsor Hickman place as being near the long-disappeared poorhouse; now it forms the core of the Elizabeth Lakes neighborhood. In 1865, the Thirteenth Amendment set free the thirty-odd slaves who had made the farm prosperous. The next generation of Hickmans understood what this meant and moved into Hampton, the two boys becoming grocers and brickmakers and three of the girls making extremely advantageous marriages to prosperous, energetic local entrepreneurs (bankers Henry and George Schmelz and crabmeat king James McMenamin). My own Holt grandfather built his turn-of-the-twentieth-century home on the rubble left from Hickman's Brick Yard, which had provided much rebuilding material for the town.

Alice has deftly and pleasantly woven her family stories into the area's history, focusing primarily on the period from 1860 to 1910. Sometimes through lengthy digressions, she tells of the Virginia Secession Convention and the terrible war that followed, the slow but steady and ultimately successful rebuilding of the community afterward, the growth of the local black community in freedom (including the development of Hampton Institute, now Hampton University), the appearance and growth of the National Soldiers' Home, local public education before and after the war, the development of the seafood industry and changes in local lifestyles and relations during the Reconstruction and Progressive eras. An excellent chapter deals with Hampton's celebration of Virginia's 300th anniversary in 1907. Complicated and comprehensive, with standard published accounts and at times primary sources, this history is fresh, interesting and extremely well told, though a bit weak on the fighting that occurred when white residents came home to find black families occupying Hampton and on the political machines and infighting characteristic of the era in Virginia. Alice nicely emphasizes harmony rather than dissonance. I think you are in for a real treat!

WYTHE HOLT
University Research Professor of Law Emeritus
University of Alabama School of Law
Coauthor of Hampton *(Arcadia Press) and* Battle of Big Bethel *(Savas Beatie LLC).*

Acknowledgements

Acknowledge:
vt. 3a: to express gratitude or obligation for; b: to take notice of; c: to make known the receipt of
—*Webster's New Collegiate Dictionary*

My acknowledgements of the people who helped bring this book to publication include all three of these definitions. I am grateful for your contributions, I want people to know who you are and I want to acknowledge what those contributions were.

First of all, there are many people who helped me along the way to actually writing this book. Will Molineux loaned me some of his own notebooks that then led me to other sources. The staff at Hampton Library, especially Liz Wilson, put me on the track of local maps and documents. The transient occupants of the Deed Book Room in the Hampton Courthouse helped a novice find her way around. Ed Morgan shared newspaper clippings as well as some stories of old Hampton. Mary Molineux and Alan Zoellner at William and Mary's Swem Library searched me out in the stacks and offered new information. Michael Cobb and Beth Austin at the Hampton History Museum provided support and many wonderful pictures. My cousin Lollie McMenamin Phillips shared pictures from her family scrapbook. I have never before written anything for publication and would have been very lost without the help and encouragement of my commissioning editor, Banks Smither.

I also want to express my appreciation to my friends and tennis partners who kindly asked me, "How is the book going?" Two of those friends were my "readers" and gave me their encouragement that the book was worth the writing. Joyce McKnight, whom I have known since college days and who still lets me call her BJi, was one of them. The other was Sandy McLeod, who brought me up-to-date on the latest Jamestown history discussion and its proper vocabulary.

There was no way I could have written this book without the help of my husband, Wayne. When either the computer or the operator was recalcitrant, he could fix the problem. He also drew the maps on the computer and found new images to consider. Wayne is an important part of the Erickson writing team.

Thank you.

Introduction

All politics is local"—that phrase was coined by Thomas P. (Tip) O'Neal when he was a member of the U.S. House of Representatives from 1953 to 1987. As Speaker, he illustrated the force of that idea by pointing out the local advantages of complex issues to opposition members of the House, thus gaining their cooperation. History is also local, even when the issues are broad and complex. People live through the events we call history, and knowing something about their lives gives us a better understanding of the immediate effects of those events, as well as an inkling of what might happen in the future. Local experience leads to local change and adaptations. This was especially true for Elizabeth City County and the town of Hampton during the Civil War and the years after that conflict. By following one family through that period, we can see something of the whole civilian experience. People who had lived along the bay, rivers and creeks for generations were related to one another, spoke with the same local accent, used the same expressions and went to school and church together. We will follow the Charles Windsor Hickman family of Elizabeth City County in this study, since in their lifestyle and relationships with the wider community, they are representative of the ordinary civilians who rode out the storm of the Civil War and its aftermath.

1

Historical Background

The Virginia Peninsula, the Hickman Farm and Fox Hill and Old Point Comfort and Its Forts

The Virginia Peninsula

The Virginia Peninsula, as the entire area is known, has been a pleasant place to live since prehistory America. Its moderate climate, plentiful seafood, arable land and available water transport made it a place to settle rather than a stopping-off point on the way to someplace else. The first Englishmen to see the land in 1607 found a well-established village of Kicotan Indians on the site. Some of the Jamestown settlers came back three years later and established a small settlement nearby, probably on what is now known as Strawberry Banks. In 1619, when the first elected General Assembly of the colony met at Jamestown, four corporations were established to include all the area settlements: "The region from the bay on both sides of the river, to Chuckatuck on the south side and to Skiffe's Creek on the north side constituted Elizabeth City Corporation, a name preferred by the inhabitants to the heathen name of 'Kicotan' and bestowed in honor of King James' daughter Elizabeth."[1]

In March 1622, an Indian raid killed 346 out of a total of 1,240 English men, women and children living in small settlements along the James River.[2] The people of Elizabeth City seemed to have been warned of trouble and made preparations because no one was killed there. Furthermore, "as a result of the massacre, the Indians were driven far away from the settlements, and the colony, relieved from their presence, in a few years again put on a prosperous appearance. In 1628, we are told that there was a great plenty of everything in the colony and 'peaches in abundance at Elizabeth City.'"[3] The "problem" of the Indians and their occupation of land desired by white settlers had been solved in the Virginia Colony, as the land was taken by force of arms. The peaches in Elizabeth City came at a great price.

The town of Hampton came into existence in 1680, when "the General Assembly passed an act condemning fifty acres, in each of the counties, for towns, to be centers of trade and sole places of import and export."[4] The property was divided into half-acre lots, and some were sold. The act was soon suspended but not, it turned out, for long: "In 1691 the act was revived, and the town for Elizabeth City County was decreed to be built on 'the west side of Hampton River, on the land of Mr. William Wilson, lately belonging unto Mr. Thomas Jarvis, deceased, the plantation where he late lived, and the place appointed by a former law and several dwelling houses and warehouses already built.'"[5] The town was called Hampton after the bodies of water already known by that name: Hampton River and Hampton Roads. They had been named "in honor of Henry Wriothesley, Earl of Southampton, President of the Virginia Company of London from 1620 to 1625."[6] After Jamestown ceased to exist as a town, Hampton became known as the "oldest continuous English-speaking settlement in America." Elizabeth City County is also the oldest Anglican parish, as the first minister of the new church established there was "the Reverend William Mease, or as sometimes written, Mayes or Mays. Mr. Mease is recorded as coming to Jamestown from England in 1610 and was appointed to 'Kicotan.'"[7]

By the mid-1800s, the trade in tobacco, which had been the major crop planted in the area, had diminished as the fertility of the soil was depleted from overplanting and lack of crop rotation. Hampton was no longer the busy commercial port it once had been, but things were looking up: "Between 1850 and 1860 Eastern Virginia greatly improved under the new system of farming introduced by Edmund Ruffin, which restored the fertility of the overworked soil. Millions of dollars were added to the value of the lands. Hampton and Elizabeth City County shared in the prosperity, and there were fewer places in the United States where the people lived in greater comfort."[8] Farmers now grew wheat, corn and vegetables and raised livestock. The waterfront was still a source of livelihood and a drawing card for tourists at the Hygeia Hotel at Old Point Comfort.

By 1860, the population of Hampton and Elizabeth City County included 4,173 white citizens, 274 free black residents and 3,199 slaves.[9] These are the people we will follow through the next fifty years.

POPULATION OF ELIZABETH CITY COUNTY AND HAMPTON VIRGINIA[10]

Year	Total	Black Slaves	Free Black Population	White Population
Elizabeth City County				
1791	3,450	1,876	18	1,556
1800	2,778	1,522	18	1,238
1810	3,598	1,734	75	1,789
1840	3,706	1,708	49	1,954
1860	5,798	2,417	201	3,180
Hampton				
1860	1,848	782	73	993

THE HICKMAN FARM AND FOX HILL

People in Elizabeth City County lived on farms, not plantations. There were no grand manor houses with spreading green lawns. The Hickman farm is marked on maps of that period as being on the south side of Fox Hill Road near where Harris Creek Road comes in.[11] It was a white-frame two-story house set back somewhat from the road, with all the usual outbuildings scattered across the rear of the property. The farm came into the family when William Hickman bought 147 acres from the Armistead Tract in 1842. His son Charles Windsor Hickman[12] began adding to the property in October 1848 with 160 acres, called "Toppings," and then another 30 acres bought from Jefferson Phillips. In 1854, Charles paid off a bank loan of $949.57 on 338 acres on the Main (Fox Hill) Road. By 1860, he owned a farm of 675 acres,[13] which he called Pleasantville. The name implies a certain air of harmony, which seems appropriate for the family that came to inhabit it. They would need that background of harmony and optimism as they began their new lives after the devastation of the Civil War that was soon to come. Jefferson Phillips owned the farm just to the west of the Hickman property, and Fox Hill Village was just one and three-quarters miles to the east.

The village of Fox Hill needs to be given its own place in this history, as its people and strategic location along the edge of the Chesapeake Bay played

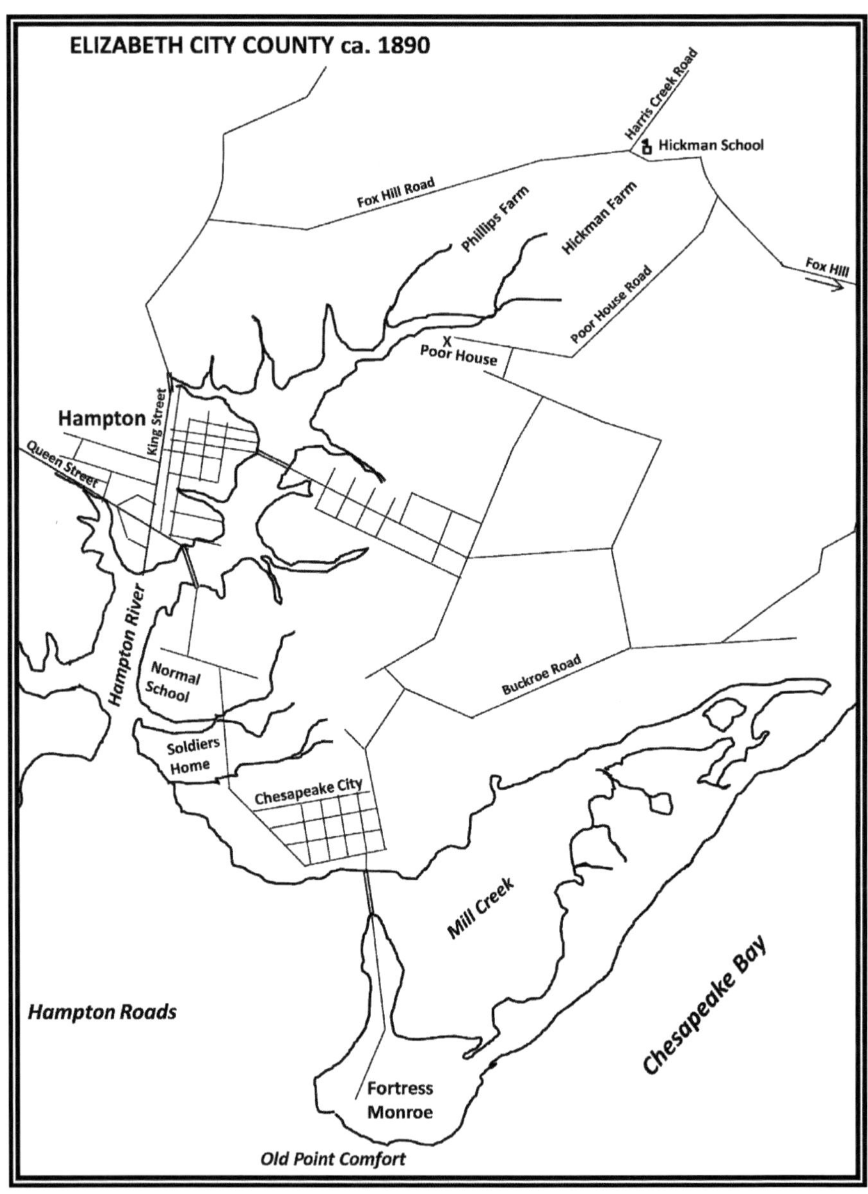

Elizabeth City County, circa 1890. The location of the Hickman farm on the map shows its proximity to Fox Hill and that the poorhouse is also in the neighborhood. The farm is not very far away from Hampton; the glow in the night sky from the burning town would have been clearly visible. The Hampton River comes up to the southern edge of the property. *Drawn and revised from map of Elizabeth City County by E.A. Semple, G3884.H2 1892 .S46, courtesy of Library of Virginia, Richmond.*

an important role in the coming conflict. People had settled in the area along Harris Creek and Back River since around 1625, but the village came into being with "a large influx of fishermen and boat builders who came from Eastern Shore and Maryland in about 1815 and settled the Fox Hill area,"[14] which was part of Elizabeth City County. William Hickman was one of those who came from Maryland, and it is his son's family that will be our guide in this undertaking. It is not known how Fox Hill acquired its name; there has been nothing resembling a hill there in recorded history. The land is marshy and threaded with small creeks around the higher, dry area of the village itself. The eastern border is the Chesapeake Bay, which must have been the enticement for those fishermen from "away."

Besides the neat, compact aspect of the village itself, there are (or were) two interesting things to note. One is the fact that there were three Methodist churches within walking distance of one another. The other is the lighthouse that was on the beach at Grand View. The Back River Lighthouse was established in 1829 and was thirty-three feet tall, made of brick and painted white. It was in operation until 1936 and could be seen three miles out to sea.[15] The storms that regularly lash the coast finally demolished the old tower in 1956. The positions

Grandview Lighthouse and Light Keeper's House. The house was protected by a seawall and was connected to the lighthouse by a pier. The structure was also known as the Back River Light and was partially destroyed in the storm of 1933. *Courtesy of Hampton History Museum, 1966.57.1.*

of lighthouse keeper and poorhouse keeper are two of the more interesting occupations listed in the census records of that day for the Fox Hill area.

The fishermen of Fox Hill engaged in what is known as pound-net fishing, which was their main occupation until the 1940s and World War II. Nets were strung along pound poles driven into the sea floor in a particular pattern. The fish swam along the nets into gradually narrower bays, until they were herded into a large net that could be tightened and pulled into a boat. The fish caught in this fashion were croakers, trout, flounder, spot and mackerel.[16] Fishermen also brought in huge sturgeon, which were "one of the first fish that the first settlers caught in large quantities because of its roe or caviar, which was salted and shipped to England."[17] Sturgeon were caught in the bay until the 1960s.

Salt production was begun along the shore between Fox Hill and Buckroe in 1776, in an area known ever since as the Salt Ponds: "John Cary was appointed manager to erect and operate a salt works in Elizabeth City County by the General Assembly of Virginia…[He] was paid two shillings a bushel for all salt produced. It sold at a rate of fifty shillings for fifty bushels. The salt was rationed at the rate of one peck for each family member [per year]."[18] Evaporation by exposure to the sun was the traditional process used here. At high tide, seawater running through a canal was allowed to flow into the first basin and then blocked off. From there it was channeled into smaller and smaller ditches and allowed to dry for a few days at each stage. Salt crystals formed as the water dried up. To hasten the evaporation process, the briny water could be ladled into large pots and heated over a hot fire. The salt thus produced would have been sold locally.

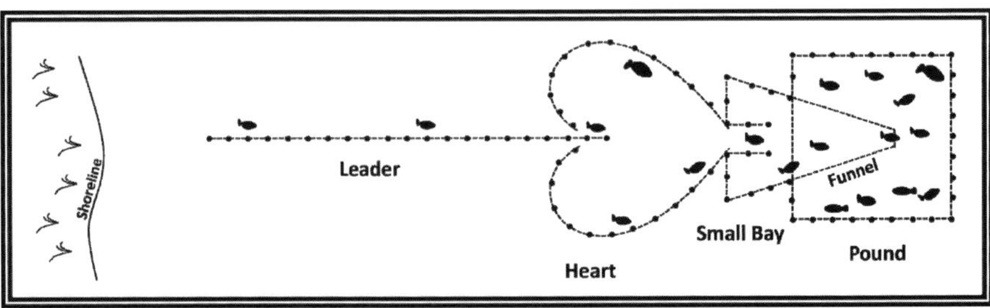

Schematic of a pound net. (1) The leader directs the fish into the heart net and then into the series of nets to the pound head. (2) The fisherman lowers one side of the pound net and rows a small boat into the pound. The end of the funnel is raised to trap the fish. (3) The large pound net is then raised, bringing the fish to the surface, where they are hand dipped into the boat. *Based in part on a sketch by Charles F. Elliott and the description from Larry S. Chowning,* Harvesting the Chesapeake.

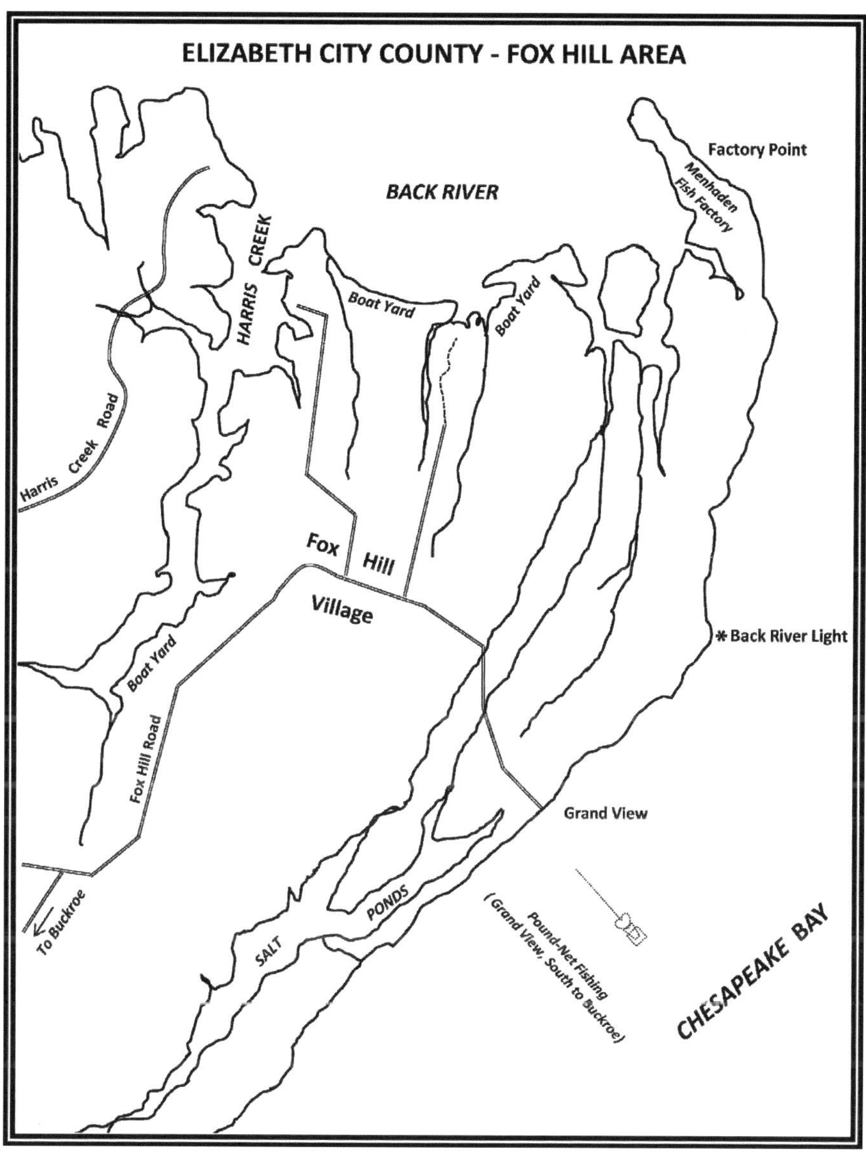

Elizabeth City County, Fox Hill area, circa 1890. Fox Hill Village is on the high ground among the many creeks in the area. The fishermen living there were close to their work but away from the storms that often lashed the shore. The entrance to the Salt Ponds from the beach is indicated at the bottom of the map. The pound nets were set offshore as shown. *Drawn and revised from map of Elizabeth City County by E.A. Semple, G3884.H2 1892 .S46, courtesy of Library of Virginia, Richmond.*

While the men of Fox Hill were mainly watermen and ship builders, the town of Hampton in 1830 had its share of doctors and lawyers, as well as clergymen, teachers and merchants selling dry goods in six stores and groceries at ten locations. There were "two taverns and three castor oil manufactories. The principle [*sic*] mechanical pursuits were shoemaking, blacksmith's work, house carpentering and ship building. [Hampton] enjoyed a considerable emolument from the money circulated by the Federal government in the building and maintenance of Fort Monroe and the Rip Raps."[19] By the time of the Civil War, the area was a prosperous, identifiable community.

OLD POINT COMFORT AND ITS FORTS

The point of land called Old Point Comfort was one of the first landmarks put down by the early explorers out of Jamestown, including Captain John Smith. It marked the safe return home for sailors who had ventured out into the Chesapeake Bay, as well as for those who were returning to the colony with much-needed provisions from England. The point was adjacent to the channel through which all ships had to travel and thus was an important location for a fortress to defend the harbor. A number of such forts were built over the years, but when the expected Spanish fleet did not materialize and no threat appeared over the horizon, those defenses were allowed to deteriorate. They fell into disrepair as funds necessary for maintenance were siphoned off to other, more immediate needs.

During the War of 1812, however, the strategic importance of Old Point Comfort was established once and for all. In June 1813, the British sailed unchallenged into Hampton Roads and launched an attack on Craney Island with the idea of taking the port of Norfolk from the water. They were foiled in this attempt by six hundred Virginia militiamen, who had been recently called into service. Seemingly angered by this defeat, the British commander took his forces across the Roads to the small town of Hampton:

> *On the 25th of June, 1813, he landed a force of 2500 men at what is now "Indian River," and with a small squadron sailed to the mouth of Hampton Creek, from which he shelled the town. The place was defended by 450 Virginia militia under Col. Crutchfield stationed at "Little England" with seven small cannon. Taken in the flank by the British land force, the small garrison had to abandon the place and retreat up the peninsula. The British*

> *occupation was attended with barbarous circumstances, the responsibility of which they afterwards ascribed to some French prisoners, who constituted a part of the British force.* [These offenses included] *the private houses that were plundered, the gray hairs that were exposed to wanton insult, the sick man that was murdered in his bed under circumstances of peculiar aggravation, the females that were publicly borne off to suffer the last degree of unutterable violence, and the house of God given over to sacrilegious outrage.*[20]

Hampton had suffered a terrible violation, but the vulnerability of the entire area surrounding what local people call "the World's Greatest Harbor" was made all too evident. Thus it was determined to build a secure fortress on the point to command the entrance to the harbor. The land was ceded to the United States government for a military post, and work was begun in 1817:

> *The Fort covers about eighty acres of ground. Its form is that of an irregular hexagon, two sides of which command the water front, while four look out upon the land. The walls, which are of granite, rise to the height of 35 feet; and about the entire work a moat extends—from seventy-five to one hundred and fifty feet wide, and faced with granite—the water in which rises to the height of 8 feet at high water. On the land side the ramparts are solid with the exception of some of the flanks which are casemated, but on the side toward the water the armament consists of two tiers of guns, one casemated and one* in barbette.[21]

The fort was completed in 1834, and as every Virginia schoolchild knows, Robert E. Lee served there as a young lieutenant during its construction. It was named Fortress Monroe after President James Monroe, who was in office at that time.

When cannons were fired during practice from Fort Monroe's channel parapets, it was found that the reach was not sufficient to

> *totally command the main shipping channel leading into Hampton Roads. Complete control of the channel could only be achieved by building a companion work to Fort Monroe on the Rip Raps. The Rip Raps consisted of a shoal located almost a mile from Old Point Comfort in the middle of the entrance to Hampton Roads. This required that engineers first create an artificial island of stone upon which a tower battery, named Fort* [or castle] *Calhoun in honor of then Secretary of War John C. Calhoun, was*

Fort Monroe, Old Point Comfort and Fort Calhoun (the Rip Raps). This is a drawing of the early years of Fort Monroe, before the Hygeia Hotel was built. The horse and cart seem to be heading home to the farm on the other side of the water. The Rip Raps are on the far right. *Courtesy of Fort Monroe's Casemate Museum.*

Fort Monroe with numerous ships. The earth-bound artist gave us a bird's-eye view of the early Fort Monroe, with mostly sailing ships in the harbor. The Segar farm is seen clearly on the right, and the entrance to Hampton River is at the upper right. *Courtesy of Fort Monroe's Casemate Museum.*

> *to be built. The project encountered serious foundation problems. It was not until 1860...that Castle Calhoun neared completion.*[22]

The name was later changed to Fort Wool, after General John Ellis Wool, who commanded Fort Monroe in 1861. To avoid confusion and to give the fort the name of its origin, local people have always called it the Rip Raps.

The fort was located on such a prime piece of property that it was soon joined by a resort hotel. The Hygeia was built to the west of the fort, overlooking the harbor, and catered to those Northerners who succumbed to such enticements as those described here:

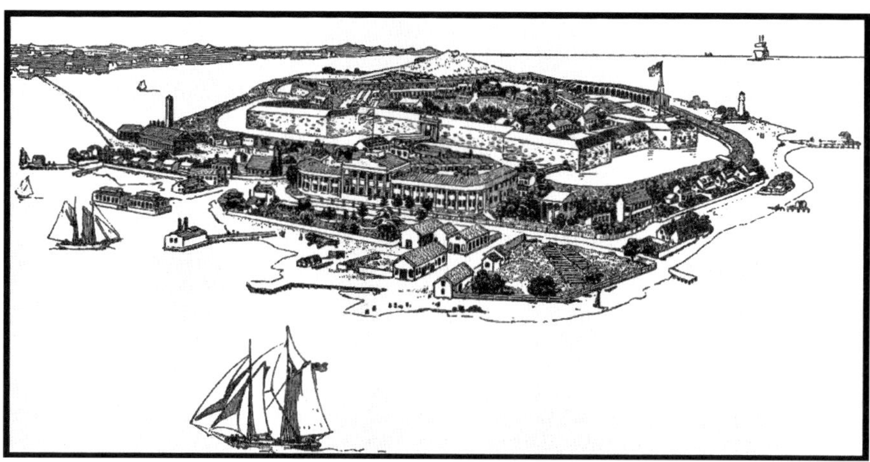

Fort Monroe and the Old Hygeia Hotel. This scene from an old lithograph represents the quiet vacation spot on the seaside that drew visitors from the North. The first Hygeia Hotel is clearly seen, as are the moat and fortress. The sand beach extending straight up from the center leads to Buckroe and the beach along the Chesapeake Bay. *Courtesy of Fort Monroe's Casemate Museum.*

> *For years before the war, Old Point Comfort had been celebrated as a watering place. The singular salubrity of its location, malarial fever being absolutely unknown, assured it a wide celebrity as a place of residence during the heated summer months. The mildness of the climate, also, aided to produce the same results. From the broad Atlantic the winds, tempered with the soft exhalations of the sea, sweep towards it, bearing coolness and tonic invigoration upon their wings. The temperature in summer ranges between 60 and 80 degrees, and the nights are few when a bed-covering is not found an agreeable necessity of repose. The gentry of the upper country flocked hither during the summer months to enjoy the unaccustomed luxury of sea bathing and fishing.*[23]

Fortress Monroe, which brought federal money and wealthy tourists to the town of Hampton, was soon to become a factor in the months-long debate over the question of secession: whether Virginia would remain with the Union or join the new Confederacy. It could be said that the fort and its reinforced garrison played a crucial role in the escalation of tensions that eventually led to a civil war. It was also an odd twist of fate that the stronghold, built to protect the town and defend the harbor, would, by its very proximity, become the reason the citizens burned their town to the ground.

2

Prologue

As an introduction to the Hickman family, who will be our guides and partners in this historical undertaking, let me say that my grandmother Angelina Hickman was the sixth child, born in 1859 on the farm in Elizabeth City County. She is an excellent illustration for this study, as she lived her entire life in the county, through the war with all of its uncertainties, and with her mother and sisters became a refugee to North Carolina. Later, her extended family played a major role in the restoration of the town of Hampton and the adaptation of new technology into the community. She is the source of the family stories I will relate throughout this history. I called her Granny and would like a new generation to know her. As I present her to you, you can get a glimpse of a nineteenth-century Hamptonian because when I knew her, she was just an older version of the person she had always been. Events and circumstances brought change over the years, but the town and its people remained recognizable until both were swamped at the advent of World War II. The military presence increased tremendously, and about half of North Carolina moved to the Peninsula as men came to work in the Newport News shipyard. We will concentrate on the earlier years when people still knew one another.

I heard Granny's stories about the Civil War when I came into the picture in 1939. Granny lived catty-cornered across the street from us. "Us" was the Matthews family at 68 Cherokee Road, Hampton, Virginia. At that time, the family consisted of Daddy, who worked at the shipyard; Mother; and the five of us children. Mother was Granny's youngest child. Aunt Rose, the oldest daughter,

had taken over management of the family property after my grandfather died at age sixty-two in 1912. Sometime in the late 1920s, the old house was taken down and two new ones built: one for income and one for Granny. She lived in the little house next to the large one called Club 55, which was rented to a group of men who worked at the Langley Aeronautical Laboratory, Langley Field, in Hampton.

By the fall of 1940, Granny was eighty years old. Over the years since my grandfather died, some family member had lived with her, but now it was left to us. My brother Bill had been staying over there at night until he left for Fork

Top: Me, circa 1940. The picture was taken in our backyard and shows the Wythe Place neighborhood in the background. The kettle on my head was used for cooking brunswick stew and for making grape jelly and fig preserves. I still use it whenever I am making a huge quantity of something. *Author's collection.*

Left: Granny, age eighty-six. This is how I remember Granny. She always wore a full-length dress with long sleeves, even in the summer. In the warm weather, the dress was made of lawn fabric. I have her cameo and treasure it. *Author's collection.*

Union to finish high school. Jimmy and Mary Louise were in college, Angeline had homework to do and I, at age five, was unencumbered with any of life's issues. So I began staying nights to "take care of Granny." I was taught to use the telephone, and I still remember all the important numbers: ours was 5882, Granny's was 6587 and Uncle Paul's was 6202. When I went to bed in the big four-poster, Granny would line up the pillows along the open side so I wouldn't fall off. One of the great things about staying overnight was getting two breakfasts: one with Granny and one when I got home. Granny's was cooked on the wood stove in the kitchen, and I helped make thin shavings for kindling from the larger sticks that were cut to precise length to fit in the firebox. There was an electric stove in the back corner of the kitchen, but Granny used it as extra storage space when the pie safe was full.

Being the oldest and the youngest in the family, Granny and I spent a lot of time together. Granny knew what to do, and I could do it. We were a great team. There was a huge pecan (pe'-kan) tree that Granny had planted in the backyard many years ago. In the fall, when the nuts were ready, Granny would boost me onto one of the limbs that hung close to the ground. I would then climb all over the tree, shaking the nuts off. We picked them up and put them in baskets in the shed behind her house. I would go up and down Cherokee Road taking orders for pecans. We weighed and bagged the nuts, and I delivered them in Jimmy's wagon. (Almost everything we younger children had, had been Jimmy's. Nothing wore out in those days.)

Having a group of research engineers living next door to Granny at Club 55 made the neighborhood more interesting. I found out much later that some of them became very well known in the aeronautics field. Mr. Harvey Allen lived there when I was little, and he later went out to California and became the director of the Ames Aeronautical Laboratory at Moffett Field. I just knew him as the man with the huge red car. He would back it up in the shade under the maple tree behind the house and spend an hour or so waxing it. I knew about washing a car because I had helped Daddy wash ours, but we never put wax on it. Perhaps that was because ours wasn't a Duesenberg.

It was during these early years, of course, that I acquired my Tidewater Virginia accent. That was our normal way of speaking. We say out, house, about and aunt correctly. We also say (or said) to-mah'-ta, pe-o'-ny and my'-o-naise. We called our spring bulbs jonquils and narcissus. I don't think I ever knew the word daffodil until I read Wordsworth in college. We also ate greens called Hanover salad. They were something like kale. Green beans were snaps or string beans. A favorite fall vegetable was the Hayman sweet potato. It is whitish instead of orange and is grown on the Eastern Shore. Since we lived along the water, we ate whatever crabs and fish we caught. We ate both hard crabs and soft crabs, and the fish were mainly flounder, spot and croaker. Later, we learned from the men at the fishermen's camp by Indian River Creek that you could actually eat the meat from the puff toads. You skinned the fish first and then took out a nice piece of meat.

Sunday dinner at our house always meant fried chicken. There were seven members of our immediate family, plus Granny, who ate most dinners with us. Very often, there was someone else for dinner, and if it was an unexpected guest, our portions immediately became smaller. One chicken has eight parts, counting the wings, which on a farm chicken are used for flying and are tough. Mother always ate the back, and I thought it was because she liked it best. Actually, the back is the ninth piece, without much meat, and she let the rest of us have the better choices. The unusual thing about the dinner concerned the family names for the chicken leg, which has two parts: the drumstick and the upper joint. I have never yet found anyone else who uses the term "upper joint," but if you know anything about the anatomy of a chicken, you will agree that the term "thigh" does not fit the piece we are talking about.

There were a number of sayings and proverbs that I heard often, for my own edification and to mark my place in the long line of family. "I've had a sufficiency, more would be a superfluity" was a great one for enlarging one's vocabulary. There was also a practical reason for its use, as explained by Frederick G. Cassidy in *American Speech* magazine:

> *Some where* [sic] *in the dim past of the early nineteenth century (as I suspect but cannot prove), our grandparents or their parents, in pursuit of the pleasures of elegance, clothed their speech, as also their corporosities, in the fashion of the times. Proper speech, being an appurtenance of good manners, they composed, and taught their children, certain formulas of polite expression fitting to such social situations as they were liable to encounter. They knew well that informality is notoriously untrustworthy, that the spur of the moment can urge a speaker to disastrous infelicities. Better far to be prepared, to have an appropriate formula fall trippingly off the tongue. Imagine, for example, the dinner guest who, having partaken of everything in sight, is being plied by his hostess to stuff himself further. Smiling assuredly, he replies, "No thank you. I have had a genteel sufficiency—any*

> *more would be superfluity." The occasion is met, the temptation resisted, and the formula has attested to the propriety of the guest's upbringing.*[24]

We used the shortened version but to the same effect.

"If wishes were horses, then beggars would ride" was another popular saying. It is an old English proverb and nursery rhyme, dating back to the sixteenth century. It was told to us when we asked for something that was extremely unlikely to happen. There were stacks of old *National Geographic* magazines in the attic that I would read on rainy days. There was one in particular about a man who had sailed around the Caribbean. The pictures were beautiful. I remember telling Mother that I wished I could go sailing there. Her reply was, "If wishes were horses, then beggars would ride."

"You have to eat a peck of dirt before you die" may sound like an excuse for not washing your hands before dinner, but we never got away with that. It was more likely to be told to us if we made too much of a fuss over some slight imperfection in whatever we were eating. Hand-washing was not essential during the day. A special treat after school was a piece of bread spread with butter, and sugar sprinkled on top. I would fold the bread over and squish it together. The bread was then a bit grayish, but that was not a problem.

"Old man Usta is dead and gone." All of these sayings came from Granny's side of the family, and we heard them most often from Mother, but this one was especially Granny's. She would smile when she said it as if to say, "And I'm old enough to know." When the conversation is centered on things, places, people or events that "used to be this, and used to be that" and when the listener is tired of the subject, a great reply is "old man Usta is dead and gone." If nothing else, there is a break in the conversation while the others try to figure out what you just said.

"Didoes catch medaloes" is probably a corruption of some Latin phrase. There was no need for a translation: we knew exactly what it meant. If I asked Mother, "What were you and Mrs. Peake talking about?" she would look at me sternly and say, "Didoes catch medaloes." I knew immediately that I should not have been listening, should not have asked about what I should not have heard and should not bring up the subject again. If anyone can figure out what the "didoes" is, I would really like to know.

During the years when Granny shared all those family sayings, she would also tell me her own stories. She would get a "remembering" look in her eyes as she talked and laughed and sang her memories. They were still very real to her. I regret that I did not ask more questions about them, but I just took it all in as perfectly normal family history. I realize now how unsettling and even dangerous those early times were for her family and for all the others who were caught up in that storm. Granny was the typical Hampton civilian during and after the event we call the Civil War, and we have her experience to learn from. In writing this history, I insert her stories into the larger, outside events as they occurred and tie them to the actual facts of time and place.

3

Life on the Farm and Free Public Schools

Granny's parents, Angelina Massenburg Hickman and Charles Windsor Hickman, were both from local families. Many of the Massenburg men were mariners and harbor pilots, who both owned their own schooners and piloted ships coming into Hampton Roads. William Hickman, Charles's father, also owned a schooner, the *Dispatch,* licensed to transport oysters in 1821.[25] Knowledge of the water and familiarity with boats has always been an asset for those living on the Peninsula, and so it was for the Hickman family. In the late 1840s, however, Charles and Angelina were recently married. They settled on the farm being developed along Fox Hill Road and began to raise a family. Mary was born in 1848, and by the outbreak of the Civil War, there were also Alice, Charles W. Jr., Martha, Georgia and Angelina. Lelia was born in 1864, and the youngest, Herbert, was born in 1866. The farm seemed to be prosperous, with horses, cattle, sheep, turkeys, grapes and certainly chickens, all part of everyday life, as attested to by Granny's stories.

Many of Granny's stories involve life on the farm, which her father was enlarging and improving. He planted live oak trees as shade for the cattle, and some of those trees are still surviving in the residential area called Elizabeth Lakes. Granny explained that the younger children had some specific jobs related to their ages and capabilities. Their father would pay them to gather the wool that the sheep had rubbed off on the fences. An even more important job was to shoo the young turkeys into the barn when a thunderstorm was coming. Otherwise, the turkeys would stand out in the rain and drown.

Family farm live oak tree, 2012. This huge live oak tree is in the yard of a property in Elizabeth Lakes, a residential area of Hampton, and is the best preserved of many still found on the old farm. *Author's collection.*

Granny had a sense of humor, which was still evident many years after the events she related. Her sister Mary loved to read, and while she was sitting down churning butter, she would take out a book. As the story became interesting, the churning became slower and slower. Suddenly she would remember what she was supposed to be doing and speed up, only to slow down again a few pages later. Granny would go through both churning motions, fast and slow and laugh at the picture she remembered. One day, the girls were all out picking grapes, and one of her sisters climbed up on a barrel to reach the top of the arbor. "The righteous shall stand and the wicked shall fall," she quoted. Just then the barrel collapsed, and down she came. Granny laughed a lot in telling that story, so I guess her sister suffered only from embarrassment.

Being from a large local family meant that there were often visits to make. Granny's mother's sister was married to George Booker, and they lived on Sherwood farm across Back River. Instead of going west and all the way around by road, the family would take the wagon out Harris Creek Road and the edge of the water. A boat was kept there so visitors could row the relatively short distance across. If someone else got there first and took the boat, all was not lost. A long pole with a white flag on top was kept on the bank. You waved the flag until someone on the other side noticed and rowed over to get you. I don't think they had many unexpected guests, but Granny liked going to visit Aunt Ann Booker.

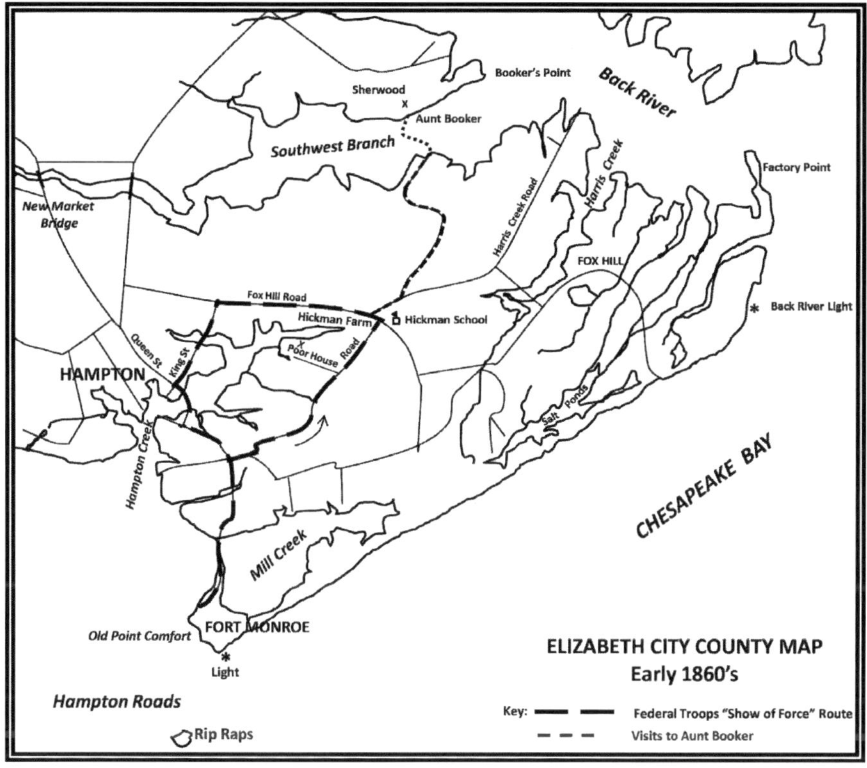

The Federal troops' "show-of-force" route and the military "picket" map put the Hickman farm in the midst of Union military activity. To visit Aunt Ann Booker, the family had to pass several picket posts (see page 65). *Drawn and revised from map of Yorktown to Williamsburg, www.loc.gov/resource/glva01.lva00177, courtesy of Library of Congress.*

Education was a concern for the parents in the area, as the only public school was in Hampton, too far away for the children to attend. Since every landowner had to pay the school tax of four dollars, the citizens of Fox Hill wanted their own school. They also knew their local history. The first free school in America had been established in Elizabeth City County for the education of its children:

> *Benjamin Sims of Virginia left the first legacy of the American Plantation for the promotion of education. By his will, made February 12, 1634–35, he gave two hundred acres on the Poquosin, a small river which enters the Chesapeake Bay, a mile or less below the mouth of the York River, with the milk and increase of eight cows, for the education and instruction of the*

> *children of the adjoining parishes of Elizabeth City and Kiquotan.—The money arising from the first increase of the cattle was to be used to build a schoolhouse, and the profits from the subsequent sales of cattle to support the teacher.*[26]

Thomas Eaton, who owned land near the head of Back River, made similar provisions in his will: "By his deed, dated September 19, 1659, he conveyed 500 acres of this land with all the houses upon it, two negroes, 12 cows and two bulls, twenty hogs, and some household furniture, for the maintenance of an able schoolmaster to educate and teach the children born within the county of Elizabeth City."[27]

By the time the Hickman children needed to be educated, the original schools had fallen into neglect, due in large part to the maintenance required for the farms, which was outside the duties of a schoolmaster. The problem was soon solved, however: "At length, in 1805, by virtue of an Act of the Legislature, the two schools were incorporated in one as the 'Hampton Academy.'"[28] This new school was located in town, on the Pee Dee Point. Children at that time were used to walking wherever they needed to go, but the trek to Hampton every day to school was a bit too much. In 1852, the public school system became countywide, and Charles Hickman was appointed school administrator.[29] A county schoolhouse was built and can be found on the Semple map (page 35) in the triangle of land between Harris Creek and Fox Hill Roads.[30] Granny talked about going across the road to school and remembered that the younger children were afraid of the schoolmaster. When he came outside during recess, they would hide behind the big girls' skirts. I guess "spare the rod and spoil the child" was one of his maxims. It is ironic that the small Hickman School survived the Civil War, while the grand Hampton Academy was burned to the ground along with most of the town in August 1861. In 1902, as part of the general restoration of Hampton, a new modern school called Syms-Eaton Academy was built on Cary Street in downtown.[31]

4

The Poorhouse and Family Responsibility

The Hickman farm property extended southward to the northeast branch of the Hampton River, across from the county poorhouse and the aptly named Poor House Road. The poorhouse was a part of everyday life in the neighborhood; there was no feeling of "Not in my backyard!" toward the institution that cared for those who had no family to care for them. In Lyon G. Tyler's *History of Hampton*, there is a brief reference that in "1760, Alexander Kennedy devised land to the poor of Elizabeth City County."[32] It is not known if the Kennedy property was used for building the home known in 1860 as the poorhouse or if the land was sold and the proceeds used for relief of the poor. Church "vestry records show that [a] poorhouse had been erected in…Elizabeth City Parish in Elizabeth City County in 1771."[33] The state church (Anglican) of the Virginia Colony was charged by law to care for the indigent and feeble members of each parish. The poorhouse act of 1755 spelled out the responsibilities of the parish vestries:

> *That it shall and may be lawful for the vestry of every parish in this colony, to order and cause to be erected, purchased or hired, one or more house or houses within their parish, for the lodging, maintaining, and employing of all such people as shall be upon the parish, or who shall desire relief from the vestry or churchwardens; and to employ all such poor persons in such works as shall be directed by the said vestry, or churchwardens; and to take and apply the benefit of their labor, for and towards their maintenance and support, and to provide cotton, hemp and other necessary materials, implements, or things, for setting*

> *the said poor to work…And the said vestry, or vestries, shall have power to purchase or rent a tract of land, whereon the said house or houses shall stand, or be erected, convenient thereto, not exceeding one hundred acres, for the use of the said poor; and to levy a reasonable allowance in their parish levies, for the education of such poor children as shall be placed in the said house or houses, until they shall be bound out according to law.*[34]

There were several other requirements in that law: the poor person had to be a member of the parish, the vestry was to appoint a "Keeper" of the house and to maintain order, and records had to be kept.[35] Those who were both poor and sick would receive attention:

> *The major duty that occupied the vestry was caring for the sick and the poor. In Elizabeth City Parish the vestry appointed Dr. Brodie to provide treatment for the poor for a number of years. When epidemics of smallpox occurred, the vestry provided a pest house, medical supplies, and even coffins when necessary for the deceased. The vestry also would "find homes for poor widows and orphans and provide an allowance to the head of the household for their needs."*[36]

Along with the American Revolution and the separation from England came the separation of church and state. The Virginia Assembly passed an act in 1785 "doing away with vestry control of the poor in all counties of the Commonwealth."[37] The county governments were now responsible for appointing a superintendent of the poor and handling the funds for the poorhouse.

The superintendent, or poorhouse keeper, received a salary and a home for himself and his family. In all likelihood, his wife acted as an unpaid assistant. "For his services the superintendent is to receive an appropriation on which to run the place. The produce of the farm belongs to the institution. What is not consumed by the inmates and staff is sold, the proceeds becoming available to the superintendent for the almshouse."[38] Those persons receiving assistance from the county were expected to assist with the upkeep of the property, as they were able to do so. When well run, the poorhouse farm could be a safe haven for those needing relief. In the mid- to late 1800s, the poorhouse along the Hampton River appeared to be just such a place.

The poorhouse occupants in the census records before the Civil War were registered as "white." Black members of the community at that time were either free and able to care for themselves, or they were slaves. There was already in place a fair degree of organization required by the state. The general assembly of 1858 established that there should be elected "by the voters of a town that provides for its poor, one overseer of the poor—for the term of four years."[39] No funds were appropriated from the state treasury for running the poorhouses, so the towns and counties took on that burden themselves.

The census records list a person in charge, called the poorhouse keeper, his family and those living in the house listed as paupers, identified by name, age and sex. In some cases, a disability, such as blindness, was also listed. In the 1850 census, the keeper, his wife and their one-year-old daughter were living on the property, and five people were receiving relief. A twenty-year-old man is listed as an "idiotic pauper." Two brothers, aged eleven and nine, and a brother and sister, aged twelve and eight, also lived in the house.[40] In the 1860 census, George T. Elliott was listed as the poorhouse keeper, and registered as paupers were two women and four children.[41]

U.S. CENSUS FOR RESIDENTS OF ELIZABETH CITY COUNTY POORHOUSE 1850, 1860 AND 1870

August 20, 1850[a]

Name	Age		
Thomas Nelson	33	M	Poorhouse Keeper
Margaret E. Nelson	23	F	
Ella B. Nelson	1	F	
George Bazurea	20	M	Pauper, Idiotic
Charles Dexter	11	M	
Type Dexter	9	M	
George Clark	12	M	
Mary Clark	8	F	

July 5, 1860[b]

Name	Age		
Geo. T. Elliott	30	M	Poorhouse Keeper
Emeline Elliott	33	F	
John I. Elliott	9	M	
Margaret R. Elliott	6	F	
George T. Elliott	4	M	
Matthew Elliott	2	M	
Mary Elliott	7/12	F	
Sarah Fulton	40	F	
Sarah Tompkins	38	F	
Johanna Tompkins	8	F	
Walter B. Tompkins	6	M	
Mary E. Tompkins	4	F	
Robert I. Tompkins	17	M	Laborer

August 26, 1870[c]

Name	Age			
Bailey Willis	36	M	W	Supt. Poor Farm
Nancy Willis	65	F	W	Keeping House
John J. Willis	11	M	W	At Home
Margaret Willis	7	F	W	
Belsey Hawkins	42	F	W	
Eliza Parker	19	F	W	
Julia Parker	1/12	M	W	
Jenny Drummond	34	F	W	
Robert Watts	86	M	B	
Matilda Smith	40	F	B	Blind
Harmon Jackson	48	M	B	
Nanny Shorter	32	F	B	
Molly Bingham	28	F	B	
Benjamin Carter	6	M	B	
Sallie Carter	6/12	F	B	
Edith Carter	52	F	B	Blind
Ellen Allen	35	F	B	Laborer
George Binder	18	M	B	Servant

[a] The Town of Hampton, Elizabeth City Co., Virginia
[b] Fox Hill District, Elizabeth City Co., Virginia
[c] Chesapeake Township, Elizabeth City Co., Virginia

The changes in the conditions of the poorer citizens of Hampton after the Civil War can be noted immediately by reading the census of 1870; the poorhouse included black occupants as well as white ones, and the number of those receiving relief had greatly increased. Bailey Willis, thirty-six, is listed as the superintendent of the poor farm, with his mother and two children living with him. Next listed are two white women and one young white woman with an infant daughter, followed by ten black residents. The black residents range in age from eighty-six to six months old and include two women who are blind and two people who go out to work: one as a laborer and one as a servant.[42]

Beginning around 1881, students from the Hampton Normal School began to hold regular Sunday school classes at the poorhouse: "After lunch [on Sunday] a preaching service was held for the whole school. At the close of that service, wagons and boats were brought into action as different groups visited the poorhouse, the jail, Little England, Slabtown, and other parts of Hampton."[43] The use of a rowboat to reach the poorhouse from the wharf at the Normal School would involve a half hour of rowing but would be more comfortable in good weather than riding in the missionary wagon along the rutted roads of postwar Hampton: "According to Miss Woolsey, an early teacher at Hampton Institute, bad roads made both walking and riding difficult. She described the roads around Hampton as being a 'bumping and thumping succession of mud holes, mended with shucks and rails and heaps of refuse and brick, dumped in and left for the wretched public to macadamize with groans.'"[44] Students were continuing to visit the poorhouse in the 1902–03 term, and as late as 1929 and 1932, they were contributing their labor on what was then called the poor farm.[45]

By 1904, the administration of relief to the poor in Virginia had been regulated statewide. The details that follow do not represent new legislation but are a compilation of laws already in effect, as reported to the U.S. Department of Commerce and Labor:

> *A person is not deemed to have a legal settlement* [declared to be destitute] *in any county or town until he has resided therein one year. Every person to be provided for by the overseer must, if practicable, be sent to the poorhouse.—Overseers or town officers must remove to the poorhouses persons who go about begging...The county poorhouse is under the management of a superintendent of the poor appointed by the board of county supervisors. A physician to attend the sick at the poorhouse may also be appointed by the*

Hampton Institute and Hampton Creek with several sailboats, Virginia Hall and Clock Tower. The couple in the rowboat are following the time-honored tradition of using the waterways to reach their destination. They could be coming from the Normal School's pier just across the Hampton River. Students used the boats to cross over to town and to the Poorhouse in good weather. *Courtesy of Hampton History Museum, 2009, 15.2419.*

> *same board. An annual detailed report is required from the superintendent—showing the number and color of inmates, the length of time each was relieved, the manner of employment, expenditures, etc. The auditor in turn makes a summary report on the poorhouses to the General Assembly.*[46] [See page 42.]

In addition to supporting official charities and church mission work, individuals such as the Hickman family exhibited a concern for others who needed quiet support. As noted in many family histories and recorded officially in the census records of the day, several generations of one family often lived together under one roof. In the 1860 census, William Hickman and his second wife were listed as living with his son Charles and family. In 1880, before any of them had children, three of the Hickman sisters and their husbands lived together in a house on Elm Street in the Pasture Point section of Hampton. This was the generally accepted situation in families.

When I was really young, someone called Cousin Adelle appeared once a year and stayed with Granny for about three months. Her husband was deceased, and they had lived "away" somewhere. He was known to me only as Dr. Ward and had been some kind of cousin to Granny. Cousin Adelle had no children and no close relatives, so she came to us for part of the year and then went on someplace else, I don't know where. While she was here she participated fully in the life of the entire family, from cooking, to gardening, to visiting with other relatives. She read *Hiawatha* and *Uncle Remus* to me, and I can still remember how she would put on a different voice for

Report of the Overseers of the Poor of Elizabeth City County Respecting the Number of the Poor and the Manner and Annual Expense of Their Maintenance from June 1, 1850, to March 31, 1851[47]

Number of the poor whites maintained at the public charge and the name of each	Number of the free blacks maintained at the public charge and the name of each	Place at which the poor are assisted	Amount of poor rates levied annually for their support	Amount of donations from individuals or others	Amount of their annual expenses at the poor house	Balance remaining in the hands of the Agent subject to the order of the Overseers	Amount required to pay arrears of the past year to meet expenditures for the ensuing year	Nature of the expenditures	Number and names of those kept at the place of general reception who were engaged in work
G. Bazurea C. Dexter Type Dexter Mary Clark Geo. Clark Ch. Nox D. Hudley	None	Poor House	379.89	115.20 Proceeds of Farm	495.09	0.00	376.65	*See statement below	G. Bazurea C. Dexter Employed in tilling the Farm

*Nature of the expenditures for the benefit of the poor:

The amount paid:		
	for hire of labor on the farm	113.00
	for services of Steward	58.50
	Overseers for their services	14.00
	Clerk of the Board	20.00
	for transmitting report to Auditor	5.00
	for coffins	6.00
	for medical services	30.00
	Sheriff for his commissions	22.11
	Agent for balance due him for 1849	23.18
	for support of the poor	203.30
		495.09

Charles Nox and D. Hudley died during the year.

J.M. Willis President O.P.

Teste
Ro. A. Armistead Clk

A Copy

Teste
L.L. Howard Clk of County Court
of Elizabeth City County

The original report of which the foregoing is a copy was returned to the County Court of Elizabeth City County, January 22, 1852

L. L. Howard Clk

each character. Her relationship to our family may have been remote, but she knew she was welcome.

Sometimes even in local families where everyone knows everyone else, there is a mystery. The Hickman plot in St. John's Cemetery has a gravestone inscribed, "Rosana Hickman, born Nov. 29, 1823, died June 14, 1894." No one today knew who she was or why she came to be buried with the family. In going through the census records recently, I believe I have found the answer. Listed in the 1860 census there is a Rosana Hickman living as a servant in the William Topping household. We don't know why she chose to hire herself out as a servant rather than live with a family member, even if she was a relative three or four times removed. In those days, everyone in the household had a job to do anyway, so she could have "worked for her keep" there. We now know that when she died, the family accepted the responsibility for her burial, giving her a final resting place and a headstone identifying her as belonging to the family. People of that time and place took on the responsibility for those who, for whatever reason, needed help and a place to come home to, even if death came first. There is an old saying that "blood is thicker than water." Family really mattered. It was noted in the poorhouse records that a person receiving relief left either to live with a family member or when he or she died.

5

The Virginia Secession Convention of 1861

After Abraham Lincoln's election to the presidency in November 1860, seven Southern states voted to leave the Union. Between December 20, 1860, and February 1, 1861, South Carolina, Mississippi, Florida, Alabama, Georgia, Louisiana and Texas all exercised their "right to secede." Those seven states differed from the rest of the South in the extent of their slave populations: "In 1860 this most tropical tier of U.S. states, with 46.5 percent of its inhabitants enslaved, possessed 58.5 percent of the Old South's slaves. The area grew 85 percent of Dixie's cotton, 96 percent of its sugar, and 100 percent of its rice."[48] Those statistics illustrate the labor-intensive agriculture of the lower South, requiring a large slave population. The statistics also illustrate some of the differences between these states and those of the North, which had led to verbal clashes in the U.S. Congress over slavery and the virulent antislavery publications of the abolitionists. One author wrote: "From all that I have read and heard upon the subject of whipping done by masters and overseers to slaves…I have come to the conclusion that some hundreds of *cart whips* and cowskin instruments, which I am told make the skin fly like feathers, and cut frequently to the bone, are in *perpetual daily motion* in the slave states."[49] Some in the South had answered with their own accusations of Northern hypocrisy, stating that the Northern manufacturers' money-grubbing policies led to situations where they used laborers less kindly than Southern plantation owners used slaves. Stereotypes were drawn, became fixed and hardened:

The extremists of the South, like their fellows of the North, stood thus self-convinced of their own righteousness, and of the depravity of their opponents. Argument had deepened prejudices. Unreason had engendered unreason. Emphasis on faults had obliterated all understanding of virtues in other ways of life. The purposes of men had become the purposes of God.[50]

In the midst of all this rancor, and by the beginning of 1861, the people of Virginia realized that they had to make some decisions regarding their relationship with the Union called the United States of America. The legislature called a special convocation, the Virginia Secession Convention, to discuss the matter and to make recommendations to be sent to the people. Many of the speeches made on the floor of the convention referred to those attitudes and policies of Northern states that were antagonistic to the South as a prime reason for leaving the Union. The Unionist delegates to the convention denied there was an irrepressible conflict that could not be resolved. The debate lasted for two months. The convention is given a great deal of attention here because the outcome profoundly changed the nation and altered forever the lives of the people living in Hampton and Elizabeth City County. Its effects, both physical and societal, would be felt for many years past the war itself. If circumstances had been different, and Virginia had remained in the Union, I believe there might not have been a sustained conflict with the Southern Confederacy. The decision was crucial and not easily come by. On the following pages, the words of the delegates themselves speak to the many issues they faced as they agonizingly worked their way through a maze of detail and differing opinions.

In February, "Virginia voters elected convention delegates, charged with recommending which nation the state should sustain,"[51] whether to stay with the Union or to join forces with the Confederate states. The voters also made clear that "a popular referendum must approve any convention ordinance."[52] Charles King Mallory, a Hampton lawyer, was elected to the Secession Convention as delegate from the district that included the counties of Elizabeth City, Warwick and York, as well as the city of Williamsburg. As the convention began, the delegates represented three identifiable positions: "Initially, around one-sixth of the representatives, almost all from the heavily enslaved east, sought immediate secession. Another approximately one-sixth of the delegates, almost all from lightly enslaved northwestern counties, sought permanent Union, even if their old nation waged war against the new Southern Confederacy. In the indeterminate middle of these determined warriors wavered two-thirds of the convention delegates, seeking Union-saving grounds that all Virginians—and all Americans—would accept peaceably."[53] Hampton and Elizabeth City County were in that moderate two-thirds of Virginians.

The question of slavery as an institution, whether or not it was legally or morally acceptable, was not at issue in the secession debates; even most Unionist speakers accepted the reality of slavery as it existed in Virginia. The question of where a property owner could take his slaves and the aggressive antislavery attitude of some Northern states were the main topics of discussion concerning the "peculiar institution." Virginia, since the decline of tobacco farming, now had a diverse system of agriculture, fewer slaves, a varied economy and fifty counties in the northwestern part of the state with no interest at all in leaving the Union. The pressure to secede came early in the convention from outside the state. Commissioners from Georgia, Mississippi and South Carolina addressed the convention in Richmond on February 18 and 19 to press the Confederacy's case for secession.[54] The Cotton Confederacy, as the newly formed nation was commonly called, now waited to see what Virginia would do in regard to disunion. The storm clouds had started to gather over the Old Dominion.

The convention in Richmond spent two months debating the question of secession. It is interesting to note that "most white Virginians cherished a crucial supposed state's right: the right of the people of a state to withdraw their consent to be governed."[55] On March 12, George Brent, delegate from the Tidewater's Alexandria City and a Unionist, spoke in an attempt to bring together the two factions in the convention. He also forcefully enunciated the basic understanding of secession: "Recognizing, as I have always done, the right of a State to secede, to judge of the violation of its rights, and to appeal to its own mode of redress, I could not uphold the Federal Government in any attempt to coerce the seceded States to bring them back into the Union."[56] Therein lay the rub for those seeking to resolve the sectional differences peacefully. Would the Lincoln government use force to recover federal property, such as forts and armories, inside the new Confederacy?

The idea that the federal government should not use coercion to bring the seceded states back into the Union was heard early and often in speeches on the convention floor. Thomas Flournoy, of Halifax County and a Unionist, offered this resolution on February 16, the fourth day of the convention:

> *Resolved, by this Convention, That whilst Virginia has a high appreciation of the blessings of the Union, and would do much and forbear much to perpetuate them, yet it feels itself bound to declare, that an identity of*

> *interest and of wrongs with the seceded States of the South would, in case of an attempted coercion by the Federal Government, demand and receive the interposition of all her military strength in resisting such aggression.*[57]

One of the secessionists' more eloquent speakers, George Richardson of Hanover, put their case before the convention on April 3 and 4:

> *Sir, let us say to these oppressors of the South..."Thus far shalt thou go and no farther." We demand stern, full and exact justice. Cease your attacks on our institutions...bow to the decision of the Supreme Court; sweep from the statutes of your States every enactment warring on our property; cease your attacks on the laws which have established slavery in places under the jurisdiction of the Federal Government; confess that we came into the Union on terms of perfect equality with you and that wherever in the common territories our flag floats, our property has the same right to protection that yours has; regard us and let your legislation regard us as equals, not tributaries...* [Then] *the seceded South may return. The Union may again stretch its grand proportions from Maine to California, from the Atlantic to the Pacific. Deny us these, our rights, and our separation from you is eternal.*[58]

The property he was speaking of was the slave population of the South, and the "oppressors of the South" were the Northern states.

John Baldwin represented the Shenandoah Valley's Augusta County and was a staunch Unionist. In April 1861, "he went to Washington in an effort to find grounds of accommodation between Virginia and the federal government, and had a private conference with Abraham Lincoln."[59] Before that secret visit to Washington, he gave a long speech on the convention floor in March, where he answered the secessionists' claims that there was an "irrepressible conflict" between the people of the North and the South concerning slavery: "[But] is this irrepressible conflict a living thing?...We have in the last Congress this remarkable fact, that will not be controverted, that by a vote of two thirds of both Houses, they have, with a Republican majority, in each passed and propounded for ratification by the States of the Union, a constitutional amendment...by which it is provided that the Constitution never shall be amended so as to give the right to the General Government to interfere with slavery in the States, in any respect whatever."[60]

He goes on to answer the assertion that Virginia would be better off by joining with her sister states to the South:

I deny the assertion that we are in any sense dependent for our policy upon them. I deny that it is either a physical, after their destiny, moral, or commercial necessity, that we shall follow their fortunes. I deny that we are so "hitched on" to them as to be "dragged." I hope, and I will not abandon that hope, that some day or other, sooner or later, the people of these States will see... [that] *with all the talk about the glory of a Southern Confederacy, with all the talk about the splendors of a Confederacy...it is after all but a Southern Confederacy, which is to have but half a continent; and those of us who have lived under the glorious Confederacy of these United States, embracing a whole continent, may well refuse to go into ecstasies of admiration over the proposition to become members of a dismembered half, aye, less than half, of a continent.*[61]

Unfortunately, there were references to a presumed racial inequality, from both sides of the slavery issue, during the general debate:

We have pontine [marshy] *districts* [in Virginia] *highly productive, but unhealthy for the white man, where the negro is impervious to the local diseases and cultivates the soil with impunity. We have the manipulations of agriculture, and some of the courser processes of mining, where the small intelligence and power of endurance of the negro come into play, but where the white man would be misplaced, and would be withdrawn from occupations more suited to his superior intellect.*[62]

These allusions to racial inequality were often followed in speeches from some of the secessionists by fear mongering and inflammatory language concerning possible slave revolts. It is not clear how those fears would be assuaged by joining the Confederacy, and none of the latter tactics seemed to change anyone's mind.

In addition to the practical and economic issues of slavery, the new tariff laws, deemed harmful to the South, and the competition for Virginia's industry from Northern manufacturers, were also argued in the secessionists' speeches and were answered by the Unionists. The debate meandered on through March and into April. The prospect of disunion weighed heavily on the moderates, and any final decision was delayed while there was still hope for a peaceful resolution.

The secessionists drew an attractive picture of the Confederate States as a home for Virginia and contrasted it with the unwholesome aspect of remaining with the Union: "Where are you most likely to get a satisfactory response?...Under a government bitterly hostile to you; a government... broken down in all its departments; broken down in every respect?...Do you want to...remain under this Washington government, when you see an efficient and friendly government imploring you to join them; a government that is infinitely stronger even at this time?...And it grows stronger every day."[63]

The withdrawal of Virginia from the Union was often portrayed as a simple matter of notifying the Federal government of the decision and then arranging a meeting with the state's representatives at a later date to negotiate treaties between equal nations. There would be no war.[64] Hugh Nelson, of the Shenandoah Valley's Clarke County and a Union man, gave one of only a few realistic predictions of the outcome of secession:

> *Sir, gentlemen on this floor have intimated that even the ladies of Virginia are far ahead of the Union party of this body in their zeal for war; and I have heard it stated, that in one county the ladies had held a meeting and resolved, that they would come here and teach "our hands to war and our fingers to fight"...Mothers, wives, sisters of Virginia! I doubt not that when your sons, your husbands, and your brothers are called to battle, like the Spartan mother you will tell them "to return with their shields or to return on them." But when they are brought back to you in the cold embrace of death, will it assuage your grief to reflect that you have urged them on to an unnecessary contest in a deadly civil war?*[65]

It is ironic that this man was the only convention speaker to die of wounds received in battle and that he fought for his homeland of Virginia after it had left the Union.

Thus the discussion moved back and forth, and still there was no decision. Springtime came, and March 31 was Easter. The convention did not adjourn for the religious holiday. The delegates seem to have paused only for Easter Sunday itself, and then on Monday, April 1, they picked up where they had left off on Saturday. It was noted in the preface to volume 1 of the proceedings of the convention that "only about one-fifth of the [delegates] appear to have taken prominent and active part in the day by day activities of the Convention."[66] Charles Mallory did not engage in the discussions on the floor, and by late March and early April, he was voting regularly with the secessionists. On April 4, a preliminary vote for or against secession was taken, and the decision against leaving the Union was eighty-eight to forty-five. It was reported by Mr. Critcher, of Richmond County that "I have been requested by Mr. Mallory, of Elizabeth City, to state that—if he were present, he would vote aye,"[67] in favor of secession. He was not a native of Hampton and may not have been in complete sympathy with the moderate, Unionist tradition of his neighbors. He was born in Norfolk in 1820, received his law degree from William and Mary and practiced law in Oxford, Mississippi, for several years. He "returned eventually to Virginia and settled in Hampton."[68] That sojourn in the Deep South could have shaped his ideas more than was known when he was elected as the delegate from Elizabeth City County.

Back home in Hampton, people continued their normal activities. Spring planting was finished on the county farms, the townspeople followed their usual schedules and the watermen started their busy spring season. With the onset of warmer weather, the crabs started to return to shallower water, tonging for oysters became more pleasant and the shad started their annual run up the rivers to the spawning grounds. In March, many Hampton homes would feature baked shad and shad roe for dinner.

Easter services were held in the town's churches, and the Hickman family would have been in attendance at the Baptist church on King Street. No one had any idea that this would be the last such service in those buildings. The fire in August that year would burn the town, homes, businesses and churches to the ground. Only a few brick walls of St. John's Episcopal Church would be left standing. At that time, however, nothing out of the ordinary seemed to be happening. Earlier in the year, the attention of the whole community had been focused on Fort Monroe. It was reported to the convention in Richmond on March 6 that "in regard to Fortress Monroe, there is no doubt, that since the 1st of January last, it has been put in a better condition for defense against attack from all quarters, than at any time before. Guns have been mounted upon the land side, pointing inland, a portion of the Fort which was before comparatively unprotected, and increased vigilance has been exercised in and around the Fort."[69] The reason given for this action by the military was "that the practicability of taking this post—had been discussed in the neighborhood."[70] There may have been discussion, but Hampton people knew far better than anyone else what that stronghold on their doorstep was like. Adults over the age of forty would have watched it being built, and many Hampton men likely contracted to work on the fortifications.[71] They would know better than to plan any attack. Whenever the secession delegates in Richmond talked about taking over any of the Federal properties, they never mentioned Fort Monroe. Even they knew its strength. The changes in the fort's gun emplacements were seen as a provocation, but at Easter time, there was no further change.

The Lincoln gun at Fort Monroe, 1864. It was guns such as this one that guarded the entrance to the harbor of Hampton Roads. The gun can swivel to fire in different directions, and this is what happened when cannons were repositioned to face the town of Hampton in the spring of 1861. *Library of Congress LC-DIG-ppmsca-32742.*

Back in Richmond, speeches by secessionists were more and more numerous as April progressed. There was still no numerical advantage for the cause of disunion, however, and the following speech by Chapman Stuart of the Trans-Allegheny counties of Tyler and Doddridge, in its clarity and logic, explains why that was so. Stuart owned no slaves, but took

> *the position that slavery is right, legally, morally, and in every sense of the word. But the Convention will recollect that the sentiment of the whole civilized world, at this day, is arrayed against the institution of slavery, and it is nothing but the prestige and power of the General Government now that guarantees to the slaveholder his right…By pursuing this course* [of secession], *you will, in my humble opinion, drive from us our heretofore best and truest friends, and unite them in one solid mass against our institutions. Then we will have the whole world arrayed in sentiment against our institutions; with a power right on our borders three times our strength, made our enemies by our own acts. Can we expect our friends in the North to stand by us after we destroyed our common Government and brought ruin upon them? It is hopeless to expect so. Then I hold that*

> *secession or revolution is no remedy for the evils complained of, but will tend as an aggravation of them, and will, if persisted in, lead to the extermination of slavery.*[72]

On April 4, the day before Stuart's speech, "the state's convention voted 88–45 against immediate secession. But the two-to-one margin for the Unionists could easily be reversed. A controlling block of conditional Unionists would switch sides unless the crisis generated their desired conditions. The conditions ranged from a successful border conference, to adequate Northern concessions on slavery to, above all else, no federal coercion of the Confederacy."[73] Meanwhile, the Federal fort just outside the harbor of Charleston had been blockaded by the South Carolina militia since the preceding December. Food and supplies at Fort Sumter were now running low. "After debating about the policy with his new cabinet, [President] Lincoln sent a dispatch to the governor of South Carolina on April 6. Federal ships, the president said, would attempt to supply Fort Sumter with provisions only, and as long as those ships met no resistance, the federal government would not 'throw in men, arms, or ammunition' without further notice, unless the fort was attacked."[74] There on the coast of South Carolina was the tinder waiting for the match to start the conflagration that would become the Civil War.

In the midst of this uncertainty, President Lincoln sent to Virginia for a well-known Union man to come to Washington for a secret meeting. The Unionist directly asked for, George W. Summers, was tied up in convention affairs. John Baldwin was selected by his associates for the mission and left immediately for Washington. There is no official record of the meeting between Baldwin and President Lincoln, but it was known to have taken place on the morning of April 4. John Baldwin was back in Richmond to attend the convention on the next day. The meeting in Washington had been initiated by the president and was deemed to be secret, so the results were reported only to those men who knew of it.[75] Baldwin would have communicated to the president that both sides in the Virginia secession debate agreed on one outstanding principle that there would be no coercion on the part of the Federal government to bring the seceded states back into the Union. If Fort Sumter was reinforced, the Unionist majority in Virginia would evaporate. That understanding was already well known in Washington.

> *John A. Gilmer of North Carolina who had been offered a place in the Lincoln cabinet as an overture of peace to Southern Unionists was a constant, and*

> *thoroughly informed, correspondent of* [Secretary of State] *Seward, and kept him posted as to Southern feeling, the necessity of avoiding any possibility of conflict, and the desire of the extreme secessionists that a clash should occur in order that the border states might be carried into secession and the independence of the Southern Confederacy assured. Seward did not lack other correspondents and agents at the South and realized the part that Fort Sumter was playing in the attitude of the border states. Both policy and necessity seemed to make evacuation inevitable.*[76]

In Richmond, the Virginia delegates were growing testy over the prolonged wrangling and yet continued the discussion: "Mr. Early [of Franklin County]—'I am sorry to trespass upon the patience of the Convention, which, I am sure, has already been exhausted; but, occupying the position that I do, I feel compelled to submit some remarks upon the proposition offered by the gentleman from Fauquier.'"[77] Later that day, Mr. Early and Mr. Goode of Mecklenburg County traded verbal barbs and almost came to the point of physical blows.[78] Tensions rose further as unconfirmed rumors came across the telegraph wires that Fort Sumter had been fired on. The reality of war was becoming obvious to all the delegates, though some temporized over immediate secession. Robert Scott, a Unionist, asked, "But when we secede what will be our condition? The enemy will be in possession of Harpers Ferry, of Fortress Monroe, of Fort Calhoun and of the Gosport Navy Yard; and our harbors will be blockaded. In what manner will we obtain supplies?"[79] The opposite opinion came quickly from George Wythe Randolph: "My humble belief is, that a bold, manly, decided course [of secession] will operate a moral influence upon the North that will bring them to a stand until mediation comes between. But if we give way, the storm will burst upon us and destroy us."[80]

In an attempt to learn what President Lincoln determined to do about the forts, the Virginia Convention, on April 8, sent a commission of three men to ask for that information. A terrible rainstorm delayed the visit, and by the time the men gained an audience with the president on the morning of April 13, the question was moot; the news of Fort Sumter was all over the telegraph wires. Their report would not be given to the convention until Monday, April 15, and confirmed what was by then a reality. President Lincoln's official reply included these words: "If, as now appears to be true,—an unprovoked assault has been made upon Fort Sumter, I shall hold myself at liberty to repossess, if I can, like places which had been seized before the Government was devolved upon me. And, in any event, I shall to the best of my ability, repel force by force."[81]

The tempo of the convention picked up on that same Saturday, April 13, with official news of Fort Sumter, relayed from Virginia governor John Letcher:

> *Charleston, S.C., April 13th, 1861*
> *To Governor Letcher*
> *Received your dispatch. It is true that Fort Sumter was bombarded all day yesterday, after refusing to evacuate, and four vessels were off the bar with troops and supplies waiting for the tide to come in, and the Fort was in signal with them.—The Fort was furious in its fire on us.—Our shells fall freely in the Fort.—We will take the Fort.—We can sink the fleet if they attempt to enter the channel. If they land elsewhere we can whip them.—The war is commenced, and we will triumph or perish. This is my answer to you. Please let me know what Virginia will do, as I telegraph to you candidly.*
>
> *F.W. Pickens*[82]

Each side of the Fort Sumter issue claimed that the other had provoked the resulting battle. That argument continues to this day. Regardless of the starting point, Governor Pickens was right; the war had commenced.

On Tuesday, April 16, Governor Letcher advised the convention that he had received a dispatch from the United States secretary of war. Virginia was required to detach immediately three regiments of militia, or 3,500 troops, "to execute the laws of the Union, suppress insurrections, [and] repel invasions."[83] The next day was the turning point in the convention. On April 17, Governor Letcher informed the Federal government that "the militia of Virginia will not be furnished to the powers at Washington, for any such use or purpose as they have in view."[84] Despite the fact that he had absolutely no authority to order the Virginia militia to go anywhere, former governor Henry Wise intimated that he had sent the militia to the Gosport Navy Yard and the arsenal at Harpers Ferry:

> *I know the fact, as well as I can know it without being present at either time or place—that the harbor of Norfolk has been obstructed last night by the sinking of vessels.—a force is on its way to Harpers Ferry to prevent the reinforcement of the Federal troops at that point.—to back our own citizens*

> *and to protect our lives and our arms.—In the midst of a scene like this, when an attempt is made by our troops to capture the navy yard, and seize the Armory at Harpers Ferry, we are here indulging in foolish debates, the only result of which must be delay, and, perhaps, ruin.*[85]

That argument of "military necessity" was immediately countered by John Baldwin's appeal to constitutional responsibility: "But, sir, I am speaking here as the representative of the people in a constitutional government, in regard to an act which the people themselves, by a majority of 60,000, directed should not be consummated without their voice at the polls.—I do not know the fact, that any portion of the people of Virginia have undertaken to assume the responsibility of making war, or opening hostilities."[86]

The discussion continued, but the outcome was now evident. The one criterion that everyone had agreed on, no coercive force by the Federal government, had been abrogated. The preemptive strike at Harpers Ferry and the navy yard, and the cry that "war is upon us," had the desired effect. Hampton's Charles K. Mallory had been absent from the convention due to illness since April 13, but he returned to the floor when the call went out from

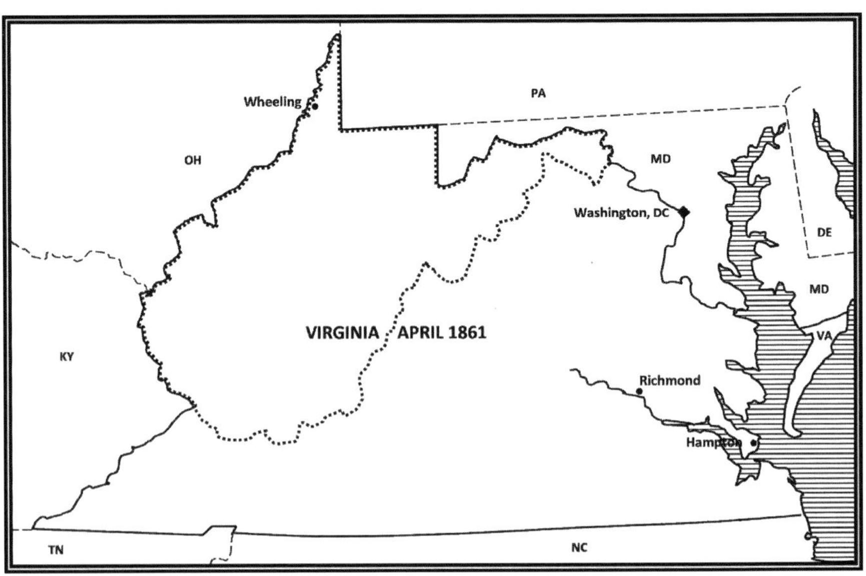

Virginia in April 1861. The broken line indicates the separation of the western counties from the state of Virginia after the secession decision in April 1861. Those counties became the state of West Virginia in 1863. You can see clearly the emerging shapes of the two present-day states. *Drawn and revised from 1850 map of Virginia, www.lva.virginia.gov/public/wv/map.htm, courtesy of Library of Virginia, Richmond.*

the sergeant at arms for "all the sick members to be present if possible."[87] Later that same day, the ordinance of secession was adopted by a vote of eighty-eight to fifty-five, with Charles Mallory voting "Aye."[88] The official resolution stated that "this ordinance shall take effect and be an act of this day when ratified by a majority of the votes of the people of this State, cast at a poll to be taken thereon on the fourth Thursday in May next."[89] John Baldwin, and other Unionists like him, would put their differences behind them, and take their stand with their homeland in the coming conflict. Baldwin told the convention, "When I am overruled, and the act of the State is determined, then comes the time for united action upon the results—, and then I shall be found sharing the fortunes of Virginia."[90]

War had come, and no one could have foreseen all of the terrible consequences; 620,000 men would be killed, including over 31,000 Virginians; many thousands more were wounded or maimed; families were displaced. Armies of both sides moved back and forth across Virginia, destroying farmland and preventing the planting of crops. Wooden fences used to keep livestock in pastures and wildlife out of gardens were taken down and used for firewood by soldiers of both armies for cooking meals and keeping warm through four long, cold winters. Towns and cities were burned. The Hickman family and all the residents of Hampton and Elizabeth City County would live under Federal occupation for four years. War had definitely come.

6

Wartime

The Civil War came to the Peninsula in a piecemeal fashion. The storm that had developed off South Carolina now moved up the coast to Hampton Roads Harbor and its tributary rivers. Elizabeth City County and the town of Hampton had been put on the alert in late winter when some of the big guns at Fort Monroe were repositioned to the land side, in the direction of the town. Nothing else happened for a while, until the Richmond convention passed the Ordinance of Secession on April 17. After that, the attention of Hamptonians was again focused on Fort Monroe; they knew that whatever the war would bring them, it would come from that direction. The fort was vital to the defense of the harbor, and the Federal fleet would need access to the James River and the approach to Richmond:

> *Fort Monroe's commanding officer in spring 1861 was Lieutenant Colonel Justin Dimick.*—[He] *concentrated on strengthening Fort Monroe, requesting troops, rations and ordinance. By mid-May the fort had been reinforced with the 3rd and 4th Massachusetts and the 1st Vermont regiments, numbering over 2,100 men and officers. U.S. Army Commander-in-Chief Lieutenant General Winfield Scott wrote that "Fort Monroe is by far the most secure post now in the possession of the U.S., against any attack that can possibly be made upon it.*[91]

Events occurred in rapid succession as the month of May progressed: "With his troop strength rapidly increasing, Col. Dimick informed the local militia commander, Colonel Charles King Mallory, on May 13 that he intended to take possession of a well on the Elizabeth City County side of Mill Creek. That day elements of the recently arrived 4th Massachusetts Regiment occupied both the Mill Creek Bridge and the Clark Farm."[92] The situation was now clear; the area was under Federal occupation.

Benjamin Stoddert Ewell, now a major in the Army of Virginia, met with Colonel Dimick on May 14 and "ordered local volunteers to withdraw a half mile from Fort Monroe to avoid any violence."[93] Hampton citizens were used to having good relations with their neighbors at Fort Monroe. Officers' wives had shopped in town, and their families worshipped in the town's churches and enjoyed the pleasures of the area. This new atmosphere of enmity was unsettling and probably brought home to them as much as anything the fact that the war had begun. Major Ewell recognized that the volunteer militia of Hampton would be no match for the reinforced Federal troops: "He concluded that Hampton could not be defended. 'It is difficult to manage Hampton,' Ewell reported to headquarters in Richmond. 'The people are excitable and brave even to rashness and are unwilling to seem to give way. It might, on the approach in force of the Federal troops, be evacuated by the military and the remaining citizens ought to make terms.' Hampton civilians could either flee with the Southern troops or accept federal occupation."[94]

On May 18, Major General Benjamin Franklin Butler was appointed commander of Fort Monroe, and by May 20 his "entire command numbered 4,451 men and officers."[95] On May 23, the day appointed for the citizens of Virginia to vote on the Ordinance of Secession, Butler decided to send Colonel J. Wolcott Phelps and the First Vermont Regiment into Hampton to reconnoiter. A small Confederate camp of only 130 poorly armed men under the leadership of Major John Baytop Cary

> *retreated from Hampton as the 1st Vermont marched into town. The town was in an uproar, despite most of its citizens being Unionist in sentiment prior to the war, as the Federal troops congregated at the intersection of King and Queen Streets.—Phelps closed the polls, thinking this might end the secessionist movement in Hampton, and then marched his men back to Fort Monroe. As Cary's men returned to Hampton, the polls were reopened and the Ordinance of Secession was passed 360 to 6.*[96]

The ordinance was ratified on that same day by the citizens of Virginia by a vote of 132,207 to 37,451.[97]

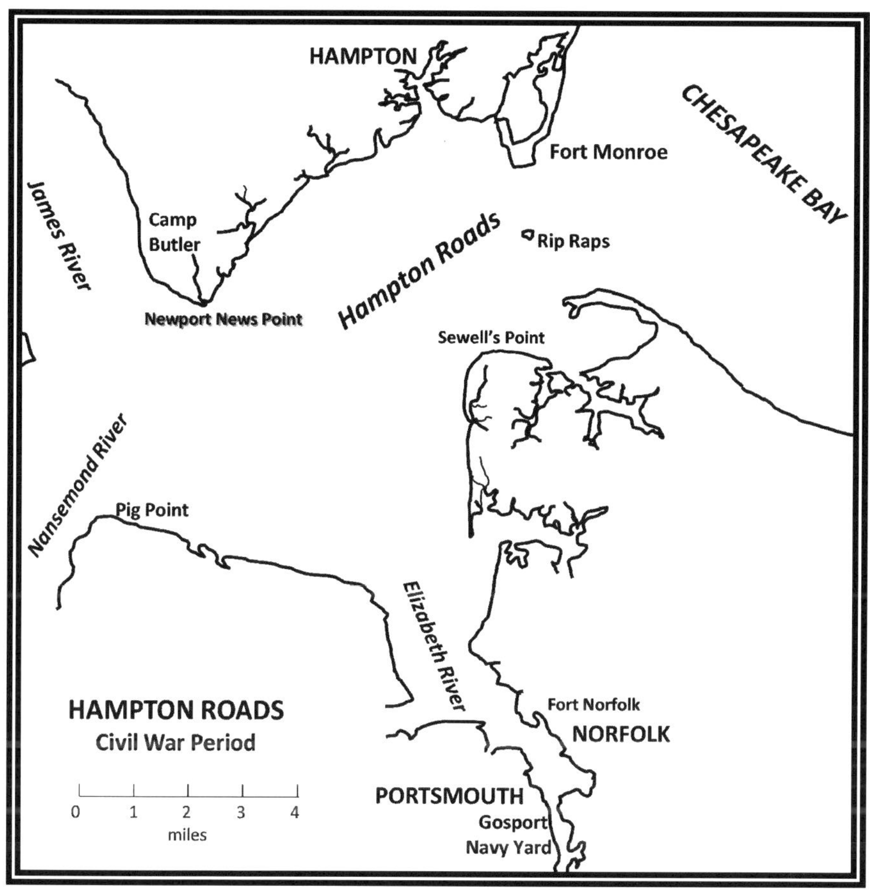

Hampton Roads in the Civil War period. This map shows the area observed by LaMontain from his balloon. He was able to see the Confederate forces at Sewell's Point across from Fort Monroe and all the way west to Pig's Point at the mouth of the Nansemond River. With Union forces occupying the military bases of Fort Monroe, Camp Butler and Gosport Navy Yard, the Federal government controlled the entire Hampton Roads harbor. *Drawn and revised from map entitled Neighborhood of Fort Monroe & Norfolk Harbor, Virginia, www.loc.gov/item/ocm54496926, courtesy of Library of Congress.*

On May 27, 1861, General Butler expanded the territory under Federal control by taking Newport News Point, and by May 1862, Federal troops had taken Gosport Navy Yard and the city of Norfolk on the south side of Hampton Roads. The U.S. Navy now controlled the entire Hampton Roads Harbor.[98]

The night of May 24, 1861, has become known as the turning point in the rationale for the war. On that night, "three slave men fled across the causeway that led from Old Point Comfort to Fortress Monroe and appealed for sanctuary."[99] The next day, General Butler "questioned the three fugitives and found they had run away because their master meant to take them along in his flight to North Carolina with the Confederate army. The three slaves would have to leave their wives and families behind. After pondering this information, Butler struck upon a shrewd plan that turned Southerners' insistence that slaves were chattel property—just like pigs or cows—upon its head. The three fugitives, Butler decreed, were 'contraband of war,' enemy property that could be employed in waging war against the Union. Under his wartime powers, Butler had the right to seize such property so as to deny its use to the enemy."[100] After that night, the realization that freedom could be gained by fleeing to Fort Monroe took hold, and many more slaves, including women and children, would follow. It is interesting to note that these first "contrabands" were slaves owned by Charles King Mallory.

Early in that summer of 1861, many Hampton residents left for what they thought would be a temporary visit with relatives until things settled down, but the disruptions in their lives were just beginning. The steamboats that had made daily stops at Old Point Comfort's deepwater wharf stopped running.[101] Then the area's labor force was depleted as black men began to flee their slave owners. They found refuge at Fort Monroe, but overcrowding quickly became an acute problem. "With over nine hundred fugitives in their fort by the end of July 1861, Union soldiers and black families took over sections of the abandoned town of Hampton"[102] and set up temporary living quarters.

General John B. Magruder was in command of the Confederate forces on the Peninsula. "On the 7th of August [1861] General Magruder determined to burn Hampton to prevent the Yankees and Negroes from occupying the houses. Messages were sent to warn the people to get out of town...Old Dominion Dragoons, Captain [Jefferson C.] Phillips; Charles City Troop, Captain [Robert] Douthart; York Rangers, Captain [Jefferson] Sinclair, [were sent] to do the firing."[103] All told, "five brick churches and another not brick, twenty-eight brick residences, twenty-six business places, [and] a large number of handsome wooden dwellings"[104] were burned that night. With no place to live, more Hampton people left for comparative safety up the James River, which was still controlled by the Confederates. They went to Williamsburg, City Point, Petersburg and Richmond.[105]

Granny's family lived out in the country and was not immediately affected by the evacuation, but the family stories include seeing the glow in the sky that memorable night when Hampton was burned to

Ruins at Hampton, Virginia. This picture is of the south end of King Street after the fire in August 1861. Weeds have started to grow among the ruins, and there is an air of desolation about the place. The once busy wharf was just to the right of this area. *Courtesy of Library of Congress, LC-USZ62-103066.*

the ground. Many years later, Aunt Rose would bemoan the fact that "Colonel" Philips burned the town, so sometime between 1861 and his death, Captain Phillips was promoted.

A military fort in the middle of a war is no place for a fashionable hotel, so the Hygeia was "partially converted into a hospital, and another part was occupied by the provost guard. Nevertheless, the hotel still welcomed guests, a practice that disrupted military activities...Secretary of War Edwin Staunton telegraphed Fort Monroe's commander, Major General John Ellis Wool, on March 14, 1862. 'You are authorized...to require the immediate departure of all persons not in the service of the United States.'"[106] The handsome resort hotel was thus torn down that December. Its position to the west of the fort placed it in the way of cannon fire toward the channel into Hampton River, so it had to go. Officers' families who had traditionally lived in the fort had gone home. Wartime conditions were in evidence everywhere.

With the harbor blockade in place by mid-May 1862 and Federal troops manning the guns from Fort Monroe, civilian life was altered drastically. "John [Captain Jack] Young was an illiterate man, but of good memory and when a man asked him how he made out [during the Civil War],

Fort Monroe with troops and ships. Something of the scope of the military activity at Fort Monroe can be seen in this drawing. Troops are boarding the ships, and military cargo is ready to be loaded. Many other ships are in the harbor. *Courtesy of Fort Monroe's Casemate Museum.*

he said: 'I had a very bad time. I could not go in the woods to get wood for fires. The marauders [guerrillas] would get after me. Could not go fishing for fear the torpedoes would blow you up, or buy a barrel of flour without getting a permit.'"[107] One of the sailors from the Union ship *Monitor* wrote to his wife about a trip to Norfolk in November 1862: "I went into the store of an acquaintance from New York & saw a large placard conspicuously placed, 'No goods sold to citizens except by a special permit of the Provost Marshal.' Just think of living in a place where you were obliged to procure a pass to leave or return & a permit to buy a spool of cotton, a pound of starch or a yard of cotton cloth, pleasant ain't it?"[108] The regulations pertaining to civilians were the same in all of the occupied areas of Hampton Roads.

Some of Granny's stories deal directly with the war being drawn into the family's orbit. As a show of force, the Federal troops would march out from Fort Monroe, go up Poor House Road, turn left on Fox Hill Road and pass by her house. They would then continue west to King Street and head back through Hampton to return to Fort Monroe. Granny never referred to the Union army as "Yankees." She always called them the "Federal troops." The term "Yankee" entered the vocabulary of Tidewater residents post Margaret Mitchell and *Gone with the Wind*. By the time troops were regularly marching through the neighborhood, her family, like all civilians living in occupied territory, would need a "safe passage" permit to move about the county or to transact any business. These permits were issued by the provost marshal in Fort Monroe.[109] To obtain a permit, one had to swear allegiance to the Union. Many local people did so merely as a matter of necessity and kept their true feelings to themselves.

It was well known in the community who the true Federal loyalists were. One local man was accused of preparing "a map or chart of Fox Hill with all the roads and houses of prominent citizens marked on it…he folded it up and put it in his pocket and said he intended to give it to the Federal troops."[110] It was understood in the neighborhood that he meant to report any anti-government activity to the military authorities. The case was taken to York County, which was still in Confederate hands. There was never a trial, but he was known from that day as a Union man and was never made privy to any secrets.

Charles Hickman was not a soldier and had not been in any of the militia units before the war.[111] He seemed to be allied more with the men of Fox Hill

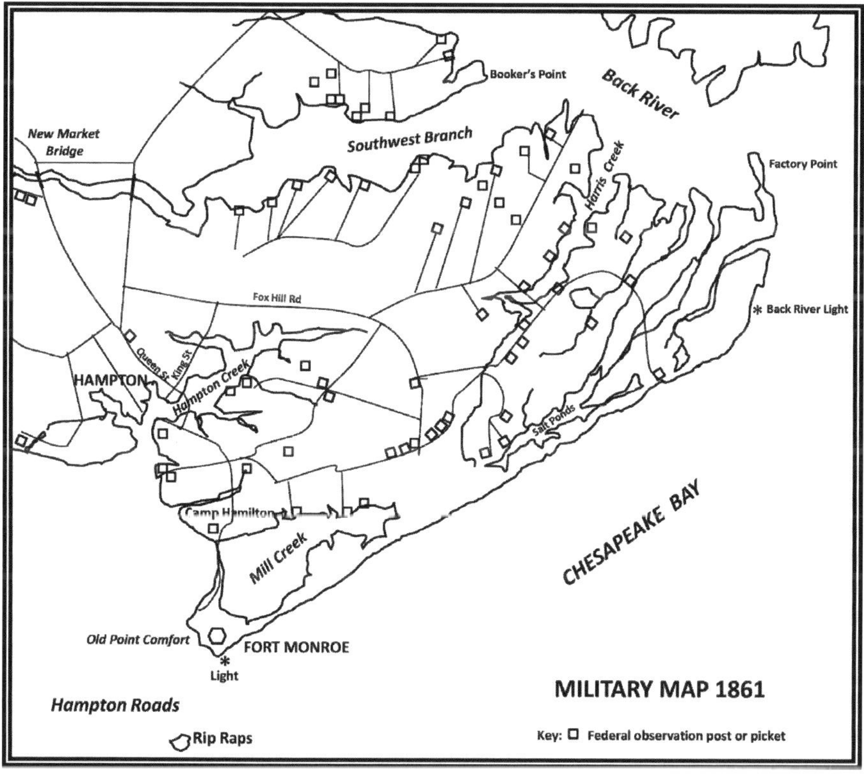

Military map, 1861. The numerous picket posts marked on the map indicate the pervasive military presence in the neighborhoods of Elizabeth City County during the four years of occupation. A civilian would be under observation wherever he went. *Drawn and revised from a map of Yorktown to Williamsburg, www.loc.gov/resource/glva01.lva00177, courtesy of Library of Congress.*

than those of Hampton, and like them, he found his own way of remaining faithful to his native state of Virginia. The Civil War maps of the Peninsula show the Union army outposts, also known as pickets, marked by small squares.[112] The pickets were very numerous along main roads and at the end of every road that led to the water. Anyone who wanted to communicate with the Confederate army would have to be a local man with a good knowledge of every creek and inlet and have access to a small, quiet boat. That description fitted a number of Fox Hill men, and they proved more than capable of gathering and relaying important information.

Yorktown, October 20, 1861
General Cooper
Adjutant-General C.S. Army

I wish this communicated to the Secretary of War immediately: Sergeant Dougherty, of the Washington Artillery, Captain Smith, at Hampton, whom I deem a very intelligent and reliable man, has reached this point from the other side of Poquosin River, and reports that he was informed late this evening by his father-in-law, who resides there, that he was from Fox Hill and ascertained that some 22 large ships of war had arrived at Old Point within the last week, also 17 gunboats; that he ascertained this fact from men living inside the enemy's pickets; that a movement was contemplated on Yorktown, with 30,000 men by land and a simultaneous movement by water with the large shipping. The gunboats were intended for the Poquosin River. Three deserters attempted to escape yesterday from Colonel Levy's regiment. Two of them were captured by my men; the other, it is supposed, made his way to the enemy. A well-executed map was found of the works at Pensacola on the person of one of them.

Very respectfully,
Chas. Mallory
Colonel, 115th Regiment Militia[113]

Virginia men going about their legitimate business in occupied territory, such as fishing in the Chesapeake Bay or selling farm produce, could pick up bits of information concerning troop and naval movements: "Any large concentrations of shipping at Fort Monroe were scrutinized very carefully and all departures quickly reported."[114] Two or three young local boys out "gawking at the soldiers" would be little noticed and possibly unseen. They could also add to the information being gathered. Granny told of her brother Charles out "spying" for the Confederates. Sometimes he would go into town with some other boys to see what was happening. On other days, they would take the rowboat out on Hampton River to go crabbing. These boyhood pursuits would be deemed harmless by the picket sentries, but reporting to adults in Fox Hill on what they had seen and heard had to be done surreptitiously. On their way back from these expeditions, Charles would stop by home and hide in a particular haystack near the house. He would tie his handkerchief to the top pole so the family would know he was there. The younger girls then carried him some food hidden in their skirts. Later, the boys would slip in to Fox Hill to give an account of their day's activity.

Another of Granny's stories was about a Confederate spy who came to the house one night during the winter. He was almost caught by the pickets and had to lie hidden in the marsh for several hours until dark. When he reached the house, Granny said he was almost frozen; he probably had what today would be called hypothermia. Her father took off the man's wet clothes, wrapped him in a blanket and then put him in the farthest corner of a room with a fire in the fireplace. He was gradually moved closer to the fire throughout the night and was well enough to leave the next day. The family did not hear from the man again, but they hoped his mission to gather information was successful.

Fort Monroe remained a hub of Union army and naval activity throughout the war. The troops assembled at the fort for the strike at Big Bethel, the two Peninsula campaigns, for the attack on Norfolk and to ensure Federal dominance in Hampton Roads. So many troops were gathered in the area that Camp Hamilton was created across Mill Creek in what is now Phoebus and grew into a tent city: "Camp Hamilton contained 5,000 residents by winter 1862. 'The white tents of the various regiments—were spread out—like toys in the distance.'"[115]

Several times during the early months of the war, a fleet was assembled at Fort Monroe to attack the Rebel forts along the coast of North and South Carolina.[116] In January 1862, a large naval expedition under the command of General Ambrose Burnside was planned to capture the forts at Hatteras Inlet, North Carolina. The fleet and an army expeditionary force were to assemble at Fort Monroe. As a convoy sailed down the Chesapeake Bay, "Fort Monroe came into view later that afternoon. Once in sight of this famous bastion of the North, ship captains opened the first of their sealed envelopes...The first envelope included the order to anchor off the fort and await further instructions. The delay in waiting for the entire armada to

Camp Hamilton, Fortress Monroe and Rip Raps. When the Federal troops' strength grew rapidly in the early stages of the war, a tent city was created across from Fort Monroe on what had been the Segar farm. This print shows the fort in the background and a fleet of ships anchored off shore. *Courtesy of Hampton History Museum, 1998.6.1.*

The great expedition, also known as the Burnside expedition. The combined army-navy expedition to take the North Carolina coastal forts assembled in Hampton Roads, with the command center at Fort Monroe. The artist made this drawing while looking at the impressive fleet from the top of the old Hygeia Hotel in January 1862. *http://hdl.loc.gov/loc.pnp/cph.3a04041, courtesy of Library of Congress, LC-USZ62-41.*

rendezvous allowed many officers and men to take a brief shore leave."[117] The order to weigh anchor came on the evening of January 11, and the fleet left the harbor.[118]

Later that year, on March 8, the Union ironclad *Monitor* came into Hampton Roads past the friendly guns at Old Point Comfort and was ready

Federal troops at Hampton. This sketch from the April 19, 1862 *Harper's Weekly* shows Federal troops moving into Hampton and setting up camp among the ruined buildings. A great deal of war material has been offloaded, and more ships are headed for the dock. The military presence in the area has rapidly increased. *Courtesy of Hampton History Museum, 1951.14.8.*

to confront the Confederate ironclad *Virginia* (*Merrimac*) the next morning.[119] At the end of the war, the final naval operation was launched from Fort Monroe. It was sent to Fort Fisher, North Carolina, to take the Confederate town of Wilmington.[120] All of this military activity happening in their town would have redefined what constituted a normal lifestyle. Civilians like Granny's family must have dealt with uncertainty on a regular basis and probably lived through many tense situations.

Even though thousands of military troops had lived in the area for four years, only a few instances of pillaging by soldiers were noted. Fortunately, the Hickman farm and the other farms along Fox Hill Road were relatively untouched, probably because they were close to the center of military activity and thus under observation. Farms in the vicinity of Big Bethel were raided in June 1861.[121] Also, on June 8, 1861, the *Macon (GA) Telegraph* newspaper reported that Federal troops out of Newport News pillaged and destroyed every farm fronting Hampton Roads in Elizabeth City County. The soldiers destroyed crops, stole or shot livestock and poultry and even took the bacon that one man had hidden.[122] Aware of the extremely bad press that would result from the raid, the Federal government put out the following press release to the *New York Times*: "Regiments at Newport News are today liberally supplied with fresh provisions, from want of which they have greatly suffered."[123] Fort Monroe was regularly supplied with provisions by boat down the Chesapeake Bay from Washington, D.C., so there was no need for the soldiers to live off the land: "During March 1862, 389 vessels would deliver to Fort Monroe and Camp Butler 121,500 men, 14,592 animals, 1,224 vehicles, 44 artillery batteries, 103 siege guns, and the enormous quantity of equipage—required for an army of such magnitude."[124]

One aspect of the Civil War that brought Hampton and Fort Monroe into prominence was the use of balloons for reconnaissance. Conditions were right early in the conflict to experiment with the wartime application of balloon technology. Fort Monroe was a secure base of operations, the Hampton Roads provided a large expanse of open territory for observation, the prevailing winds were usually steady out of the west and the general in charge of the fort was open to new ideas. It was this latter condition that brought the first balloonist to Hampton. John La Mountain had been angling for a military appointment as a balloonist without result, but his luck was about to change: "A month later, however, a welcome yet unofficial offer of employment came from an unexpected quarter. On June 5, [1861] Major General Benjamin F. Butler...wrote from Fortress Monroe, the headquarters from which he commanded the Department of Virginia, offering La Mountain employment as an aerial observer with his command."[125]

La Mountain responded that he and his apparatus would start for Virginia from his home in Troy, New York, the following week. Equipment problems and lack of funds delayed the start; the major expense was "for inflating materials amounting to about five hundred dollars. There were, he pointed out...no gas works at Fortress Monroe."[126] What he asked was "that Butler sign an order for a quantity of sulphuric acid and iron turnings, with the necessary tanks and copper pipes for the manufacture of hydrogen...In return for this assistance, La Mountain agreed to serve without pay until he should satisfy Butler of the practicability of his operations."[127]

Balloon flight was not new. The Montgolfier brothers of France had flown their huge "paper bag" filled with hot air back in June 1783, and Jacques Alexander Cesar Charles, a Parisian physicist, had used hydrogen to lift his coated silk envelope that August.[128] In September, a young French physicist "begged the Montgolfier brothers for the honor of becoming the first aerialist in history. The following month his wish was granted when he made his first flight in a tethered Montgolfier balloon."[129] The age of the aeronaut had arrived.

The production of hydrogen to carry the balloons aloft involved a chemical reaction carried out on site. A solution of sulfuric acid (H_2SO_4)

reacts with iron turnings (Fe) to produce hydrogen gas (H_2) and iron sulfate ($FeSO_4$). Because the reaction produces considerable heat, the hydrogen gas had to be cooled and purified. The balloonist's apparatus would also have to function in this capacity and thus was a rather involved system. La Mountain's baggage included all of this equipment plus his two balloons, which arrived by ship at Fort Monroe in July 1861.

His arrival was well timed; information of Confederate strength in the area was urgently needed. Being "surrounded by hostile territory and enemy forces of unknown size and disposition, with rumors and counter-rumors of enemy activity constantly reaching the garrison, made a means of reconnaissance from the air most welcome to the general in command."[130] By late July, La Mountain had his equipment ready and "went aloft from the outskirts of Hampton on the evening of July 25, thus effecting his first ascension in the service of the Government."[131] The weather was too windy at the time to get very high up, so observation was limited. After five days of difficult weather conditions, La Mountain was ready to try again on July 31:

> *He made two ascensions from the vicinity of the Fortress, the first of which was unsuccessful. In this attempt he reached an altitude of scarcely 400 feet, and descending, made adjustments and again went aloft. The second venture was productive of definite results. Ascending to a height of 1,400 feet, he was afforded an excellent opportunity for observation of Confederate activity in the vicinity within a radius of some thirty miles.*[132]

La Mountain was able to give General Butler a precise report on Confederate activity: fifty-eight tents behind the water battery on Sewall's Point, no unusual activity on the James River, a small camp behind the Pig Point battery, all quiet in the direction of Yorktown. The conclusion was: "If the report that Magruder [the Confederate general] had assembled 8,000 men [at Yorktown] was true, there was at the time of observation no evidence that this force was preparing for any active operations towards Fortress Monroe."[133] Another flight on August 1 revealed nothing new. General Butler could now make his defensive preparations based on actual reconnaissance instead of on speculation and rumor.

A special innovation in balloon flight took place in Hampton Roads on August 3, when La Mountain

> *effected his first aerial observation from the water, and in some respects may be said to have operated from the first aircraft carrier in American history.*

> *One of his balloons was inflated and placed on board the armed transport* Fanny, *and was secured to the stern by mooring ropes and a windlass. The vessel then steamed out into the channel opposite Sewall's Point, where La Mountain ascended to a 2,000 foot altitude and made a careful inspection of the Confederate position. The troops attached to the camp discovered on the 31st were seen to be actively at work erecting additional fortifications with gun pits and embrasures for pieces evidently intended to bear upon the Rip Raps, Fortress Monroe, and shipping in the Roads.*[134]

La Mountain's last flights from the vicinity of Fortress Monroe took place on August 10 and included four during the day with a "maximum elevation of 3,500 feet, higher than the aeronaut had previously attained."[135] The last flight of all took place after dark, "with no winds to break the prevailing stillness. Ascensions from the water were again decided upon, and this time the tug *Adriatic* was used as a base of operations."[136] That event must have seemed more unworldly than any other, with the darkness obscuring the earth below and silence all around.

After this ascent, La Mountain had used all the materials he had brought for making hydrogen and asked permission to return home to make further preparations for his aeronautic service to the U.S. Army. General Butler was pleased with the results of the strategic use of this new technology and signed off on La Mountain's expenses. After that, the intricate machinations of the army took hold, and everything changed. General Butler was reassigned, General Wool came to Fort Monroe and the status of the balloonist was in limbo. "In fact, Wool seems to have had no knowledge of La Mountain or of his relationship with Butler's command. He later stated that he had been given 'no instructions, and find none here [Fortress Monroe] on the subject.'"[137] La Mountain would continue his service with the U.S. government, but his rival Thaddeus Lowe would be in charge when balloons returned to Hampton.

"The Balloon Corps of the Army of the Potomac had emerged into being…supervised and technically controlled by Lowe as Chief Aeronaut."[138] The enlarged group had been operating in northern Virginia during the winter of 1861–62. In March 1862, the campaign to capture the Confederate capital of Richmond was begun, and balloons were once again called into action at Fort Monroe:

> *While arrangements for the movement of the Army of the Potomac to the Peninsula were in progress,* [General George B.] *McClellan ordered a balloon and aeronaut sent to General Wool at Fort Monroe. The mission of*

> *this unit, the last assigned before the opening of the Peninsula Campaign, was to afford means of ascertaining the movements of the dreaded Confederate ironclad* Virginia *which had recently wrought havoc among the Union warships at Hampton Roads.*[139]

The balloons were "pressed into constant duty monitoring Rebel naval activity in the Roads."[140] More aeronauts and balloons, ground assistants and equipment were placed in service with the Union army during this campaign. The Balloon Corps was now an official participant in the war.

Meanwhile, the Confederates had become more than tired of the Union surveillance from the sky, and no artillery barrage or firing by sharpshooters could bring the balloons down. In addition, the constant efforts to evade detection took up valuable time: "In the early part of 1862, the appearance of the balloons became an almost daily occurrence on front lines throughout Virginia…and soon ways were sought to counteract their presence in the sky."[141] That opportunity arrived when the Confederate army came into possession of a small balloon in the spring of 1862. It was definitely second rate in comparison with the Union aerostats, but it worked. General Magruder received a request for "an individual who was 'thoroughly acquainted' with the area surrounding the James River to perform reconnaissance duty."[142] Captain John Randolph Bryan, a desk clerk, volunteered and reported to General Joseph E. Johnston for his assignment. There had been no mention of flight duty or balloons, and Bryan was taken aback when he heard what he had volunteered for. Nonetheless, he was given a hurried lesson in wig-wag flag signals and was "briefed on the last known position and strength of the Union forces in the area."[143]

Early on the morning of April 13, 1862, Bryan made his first ascent. This balloon was inflated with hot air and had to be filled while tethered to the ground. The inflation took place when "a fire was built underneath a makeshift chimney flue, fueled with pine knots and turpentine. The balloon's valve was held open, allowing the heated air to rise up into the cotton envelope."[144] When everything was ready, except perhaps the aeronaut, the balloon rose above the trees and kept rising. "Above the battlefield, Bryan was presented with a vast panorama encompassing views of Chesapeake Bay, the York and James Rivers, Old Point Comfort, Fortress Monroe, and both the Confederate and Union fleets stationed in the surrounding waterway."[145] A second successful flight was made two days later, this time closer to Yorktown. On May 4, troops of both armies were starting to move, and information was needed by the Confederates, so Bryan, now an experienced aeronaut, was awakened early for duty. As the balloon was readied for flight and began to rise, an observer on the ground caught his foot in the ropes and was being hauled toward the windlass. Someone cut the rope with an axe, and the balloon rose on an accidental untethered flight. In spite of the unorthodox conditions, Bryan was able to make the necessary observations and came back to earth behind Confederate lines.[146]

The Confederacy tried again to create an effective balloon corps and worked on a new airship. A larger balloon, named the *Gazelle*, was made of silk-dress material and carted from South Carolina to Richmond. The new balloon was inflated with gas from the Richmond gas works and was ready for flight on July 4, 1862. The balloon was very weak, however, and came down after a short time. It was folded on the deck of the tugboat CSS *Teaser*, and the crew started to return to Richmond when the boat ran aground on a mud flat in the James River. At that time, a Union gunboat appeared, and the small boat was trapped. When the crew jumped overboard and waded to shore to evade capture, the balloon with all its equipment was confiscated. "With the capture of the *Gazelle*, balloon operations for the South were over. For all that it mattered, the Confederate air force and the future of any balloon activities for the remainder of the war were now in the hands of the Yankees."[147]

7

The Question of Slavery

The question of slavery, what should eventually be done about the "peculiar institution" and the people caught up in it, was not a topic of general discussion in early nineteenth-century Virginia:

> *In our Southern slave-holding country, the question of emancipation has never been seriously discussed in any of our legislatures, until the whole subject, under the most exciting circumstances, was during the last winter, brought up for discussion in the Virginia Legislature, and plans of partial or total abolition were earnestly pressed upon the attention of that body.*[148]

Since the subject had not been on the agenda of any previous General Assembly, why was it raised in 1832? The "exciting" events of the previous summer were still being discussed throughout the state, and rumor and exaggeration had brought the issue to the point where it could not be ignored. The slave insurrection of August 22–24 in Southampton County had left sixty-one white people, mostly women and children, dead. They had been brutally murdered. The whites of the county retaliated, and many of the slaves involved in the uprising, as well as free black citizens, were killed.[149] Rumor and fear became partners, and that marriage produced many children. What had long been true but not acknowledged openly was seen as a reality. There were a great many black people in communities throughout the state, especially in the eastern counties. There was a very real fear abroad that white residents were no longer safe from a black rebellion.

The facts of the insurrection, however, spoke of the local and isolated nature of this slave revolt. One man, a slave named Nat Turner, had been told since he was a child that he was different, marked out for an exceptional life. Nat could read and write and was extremely articulate. From his reading of the Bible, he determined that he was destined to be the one to lead his people to freedom. He talked often of his visions and preyed on the superstitious nature of the other slaves. Many accepted his evaluation of himself and were willing followers.[150] The sign to begin the mission came from heaven in the form of an eclipse of the moon in August, and Nat and his four specially selected lieutenants started the murders on their home plantation that Sunday. As they moved on to other plantations in the area, more slaves joined the group until about seventy were involved in the killing spree. By Tuesday morning, a local militia was able to end the massacre with the capture of the rebels. Nat Turner escaped and hid in a makeshift cave until his capture in October by a farmer and his dog. He gave his *Confessions* to a local lawyer before his execution on November 11, 1831.[151]

All of this was happening as delegates were preparing for the next General Assembly to begin in December. In an effort to address the issue, Virginia governor John Floyd broached the subject of emancipation in a letter to the governors of Georgia and South Carolina in the fall of 1831:

> *I shall in my annual message recommend that laws be passed—to confine the slaves to the estates of their masters—prohibit negroes from preaching—absolutely to drive from this state all free negroes—and to substitute the surplus revenues in our Treasury annually for slaves, to work for a time upon our rail roads—and* [from] *there be sent out of the country, preparatory, or rather as the first step to emancipation. These last points will of course be cautiously and tenderly managed and will be urged or delayed as your State and Georgia may be disposed to cooperate.*[152]

The governor did deliver his message, and the House received it but postponed any discussion of the slavery issue by appointing a committee to look into it. The study group was called the Select Committee on the Colored Population. Things were quiet in the legislature for a time, but in towns across the state, copies of Nat Turner's *Confessions* were sold while newspaper editors kept the issue of safety before the public.[153] The House could not keep the subject under wraps for long.

Fear for public safety did eventually bring the slavery issue before the legislature, but once the conversation started, long-held antislavery attitudes were expressed in speeches on the House floor. These speeches were answered by slaveholders from the eastern counties, and two identifiable sides developed that would argue the issue for almost two weeks. There were five basic arguments on the antislavery side: 1) Slavery created a danger to the safety of the community, 2) Slavery was economically undesirable, 3) Slavery was morally indefensible, 4) Continued existence of slavery would destroy the Federal Union and 5) "The Legislature had the authority to abolish slave property without either giving compensation to or gaining consent from the owners of that property."[154] Those who expressed opinions favoring the continuation of slavery did not portray it as a positive good but chose to answer the arguments of the abolitionists: 1) The dangers of slavery were exaggerated, and there was no evidence that the existence of slavery created the danger; 2) Slavery was not economically harmful; 3) As practiced in Virginia, slavery was consistent with the principles of morality; 4) The elimination of slavery would cause evils greater than those that already existed; and 5) Legislative action on emancipation was illegal.[155]

One thing that was missing from the speeches was a plan of action. Delegate Thomas Jefferson Randolph, grandson of Thomas Jefferson, found an opportunity to offer such a plan as an amendment to a bill on the House floor. His proposal, later known as the *post nati* plan, would provide for both emancipation and deportation:

> [The committee should] *be instructed to inquire into the expediency of submitting to the vote of the qualified voters in the several towns, cities, boroughs, and counties of this commonwealth, the propriety of providing by law that the children of all female slaves, who may be in this state, on or after the 4th of July, 1840, shall become the property of this commonwealth, the males at the age of twenty-one years, and the females at the age of eighteen, if detained by their owners within the limits of Virginia, until they shall respectively arrive at the ages aforesaid, to be hired out until the net sum arising therefrom shall be sufficient to defray the expense of their removal, beyond the limits of the United States, and that said committee have leave to report by bill or otherwise.*[156]

There had been no discussion in the legislature of any emancipation without deportation. Deportation was deemed necessary since it was thought that black men and white men could not live compatibly as equals:

> *A race of people differing from us in colour and in habits, and vastly inferior in the scale of civilization, have been increasing and spreading…until they*

> *have become intertwined and intertwisted with every fiber of society…Can these two distinct races of people now living together as master and servant, be ever separated?*[157]

The implication here is that mere separation, or emancipation, would not work. Additionally, Randolph's *post nati* plan was charged with being both impractical and unacceptable. In his review of the debate, Professor Thomas R. Dew of William and Mary College presented arguments to show that the deportation scheme would be extremely expensive. An estimated $1,380,000 would be the "expense to be annually incurred by Virginia to keep down her black population to its present amount."[158]

As the slavery question was now openly discussed on the House floor, the western counties felt free to air their grievances in relation to the fact that slaves were counted as three-fifths of a person in determining legislative representation, to the drag on the entire state of the sagging plantation economy and to the lack of attention paid to their particular interests. How the east would respond became a matter of political importance. The state legislative majority could shift depending on the outcome:

> *This section* [the east] *was thus confronted by the very practical proposition of whether or not it would surrender political power to the west, which desired greater revenues to construct roads and canals and to maintain free schools, and the power to tax the worn out lands and slave property of the east. Thus, the reform movement* [emancipation] *became complicated by problems of taxation, internal improvements, and negro slavery…But the crux of the issue was that the east possessed a large amount of slave property, while the west was practically non-slaveholding.*[159]

These same issues with the eastern counties and the Trans-Allegheny counties on opposite sides appeared again during the Secession Convention twenty-nine years later. The outcome then was a permanent separation, as is discussed in that chapter. In 1832, however, slaveholders were found on both sides of the emancipation issue. Each side won some and lost some: "On two votes coming within a short time span, the House defeated an anti-emancipation maneuver and an anti-slavery motion."[160] The House did approve a bill to provide for the deportation of free black residents and allocated $35,000 for it, but the Senate defeated the proposal by one vote.[161] Everyone had to compromise; no action was immediately available. The status quo suited the proslavery advocates, and the best that the emancipationists could hope for was "that a future legislature might consider the question again and take affirmative action."[162]

As the debate had progressed, pent-up feelings in the west had produced sharp-edged comments, and slaveholders became "more and more concerned until concern was forced into bitter opposition."[163] Governor Floyd, who had initiated the discussion in the first place, became concerned by the escalation of tension in the state and feared some kind of rift unless things calmed down. "The debate in the House is growing in interest and I fear engendering bad and party feelings. It must be checked in its erratic tendencies."[164] The moderates in the House came to the same conclusion. Even though they were themselves in favor of emancipation, "they feared that with such hostile and substantial opposition generated by the debate, it was not the appropriate time to pass or further consider the question of abolition at the 1832 session."[165]

The term "antislavery debate" has been used to describe this two-week discussion in the Virginia legislature, but it was much more than that. The initial question—what to do with the black population of the commonwealth—was still unanswered. This is where the slavery issue stood in Virginia at the outbreak of the Civil War. In the Secession Convention in the winter of 1861, the slavery question was often presented to the delegates as one of two options: join with their sister slaveholding states to the South or take the part of the Northern abolitionists. The actual break with the Union came outside that choice.

The next test of the slavery question came in May 1861, when the three slaves from Hampton appeared at the gates of Fort Monroe to ask for asylum. They were taken in as "contraband" property. After that, it became a Federal issue. President Lincoln's Emancipation Proclamation, published on September 23, 1862, "declared that upon 1 January 1863 all slaves within any state then in rebellion against the United States, 'shall be, then, thenceforward, and forever free.'—Yet it actually freed not one slave, since it applied only to rebel states where it could not be enforced. The loyal slave states, occupied New Orleans, and occupied parts of Virginia were excepted."[166] It is not known how many local slaves fled to Fort Monroe for protection, but "with each passing day after the spring of 1862, Hampton's original contraband were becoming more and more of a minority in their own black community.—The newcomers had also been slaves, but they were from counties throughout much of eastern Virginia."[167] They mostly came down the natural highways of the Peninsula, its rivers, to land at Old Point Comfort, thus giving that name a new meaning. Eventually, there were more than twenty thousand who came. It was known that food and housing resources for the contrabands were stretched thin: "With the burning of Hampton Village by Confederate forces and the large numbers of escaped slaves flocking to the area, blacks were left without adequate food, clothing or housing and suffered considerably during the fall and winter months."[168] The problems also extended to economic concerns: "An increasing number of blacks came to Old Point Comfort where they [originally] found food, employment and sanctuary. The men were used as servants to officers, cooks, stevedores, trench diggers and carpenters, while women were detailed as cooks, laundresses and chambermaids. Sadly for the contrabands, payment for services rendered was infrequent at best."[169]

Since the contrabands had appealed to the U.S. Army for protection, the army now had the responsibility of caring for them. Those who were able were put to work, but there were now women and children, as well as older adults, who needed care. In October 1861, a Special Order was issued "to formalize procedures for the care of escaped slaves. All able-bodied blacks were to be put to work...Wages were set at eight dollars a month for men and four dollars for women, plus full rations for workers and half rations for their dependents. The blacks, however, were not to receive their wages in cash. Payment was withheld to buy their clothing, and the remainder was put in a fund to provide food and clothing for those unable to work."[170] This system sounded to the black recipients a lot like the old one they had just left; they still had no actual money. It also led inevitably to abuse: "The Quartermaster's Department, charged with keeping pay records and with distributing goods to blacks, robbed them at every turn. Clothing and rations were credited to refugees but actually sold on the black market."[171]

Missionaries had come to Hampton to aid the freedmen and appealed to General Wool, commander at the fort, to address the situation. Eventually, the abuses ended for a while, and the former slaves were given a modicum of freedom: "April of 1862 brought the spring thaw and somewhat improved conditions. Blacks were given lumber to construct their own houses. Together with the missionaries, they renovated the burned-out courthouse in Hampton to use as a school and church."[172]

In July 1862, Congress passed the Second Confiscation Act, "which declared that all slaves who came within Union lines would be 'forever free of their servitude' and which authorized the president to 'employ as many persons of African American descent as he may deem necessary and proper for the suppression of this rebellion.'—Congress simultaneously passed a militia act authorizing the military's use of black laborers for 'any military

Freedmen's Village, *Harper's Weekly*, September 30, 1865. Former slaves built their cottages around the chimneys of the burned-out houses in Hampton. This area became known as the Grand Contraband Camp. *Courtesy of Hampton History Museum, 1966.1.1.*

or naval service for which they may be found competent.'"[173] At that time, the outcome of the war was definitely still in question. That uncertainty, along with word of the poor living conditions and labor required of the contrabands, would be talked of in the black community of Hampton. As a result, some slaves on the Peninsula adopted a "wait and see" attitude about leaving home.

According to the 1860 census, there were thirty slaves living on the Hickman farm. I do not know how many stayed on the farm after the war started, but I do know that Uncle Henry and his wife, Aunt Sadie, remained with the family. The terms "uncle" and "aunt" were not used in a disparaging manner, as one might suppose looking back across our latter-day history. The children on Pleasantville farm would have used those terms of respect because this black couple held responsible positions in the care of the entire household, which at this time included forty people. It would not have been proper to call them by just their first names.

"Anti-bellum blacks in Hampton experienced a slave system considerably more relaxed than elsewhere in the South. Fewer slaves in Hampton were simple fieldhands on plantations; many more slaves were permitted to 'hire their own time.' Other slaves were oystermen, fishermen, skilled craftsmen; a few were even foremen of their master's farms. A number could read and write; most had stable families."[174] In one well-known case, a slave named George Scott fled his master, who was known as a cruel and harsh man. Almost everyone in town knew where George was staying, but no one turned him in. In fact, people brought him food and even hired him to do odd jobs for them.[175] That relaxation of the usual master/slave association was the result of a relationship that had grown up over the years between people. The relationship lasted longer in Hampton than elsewhere, but the chaos of war created tensions between the white and black populations across the whole area.

Slavery was certainly an offense to the humanity of black people, and its ending was too long delayed. When emancipation did come, Hampton African Americans were more prepared than most to take advantage of their freedom. They carried the training, education and sense of responsibility gained through those years of servitude into a new lifestyle with confidence. They were now free to make their own choices.[176]

8
To Wilmington

Late in the war, when Federal troops had literally taken over the Peninsula, Granny's father decided that his wife and daughters needed to go to a safer place, just as many other families had chosen to do: "Many Southern adults lived through the war on edge, fearful for their safety, and worried about their ability to protect and provide for their children. Such fears led many Southerners to uproot themselves, while others were forced to leave.—By one historian's conservative account, at least 250,000 Southerners left their homes behind during the war years."[177] Granny's family joined that great migration away from home and all that was familiar. Some of Charles Hickman's relatives lived in Wilmington, North Carolina, which was still in Confederate hands. The question was how to get his family there. Hampton, Norfolk and the Hampton Roads Harbor were all under Federal control by May 1862, so travel with a "safe passage" permit and permission from the provost marshal at Fort Monroe would get them to Norfolk. General Butler was the commander of the Department of Virginia and North Carolina from October 1863, so any permit issued by his provost could include going south, where the family would travel. The fact that the group included no men or boys of military age, who could augment the Confederate forces, was most likely helpful in obtaining a travel permit. Some of Granny's Massenburg relatives were still licensed pilots and owned good-sized boats, so water transport was available. From Norfolk, they could go by wagon southward into North Carolina. Granny talked about going to Wilmington during the war with her mother and sisters and said that Uncle Henry and

View of Norfolk Harbor and Portsmouth. The Civil War port of Norfolk was the first destination for the Hickman family on their way to Wilmington, North Carolina. They would have come across from Hampton in a sailing schooner with a Massenburg relative as pilot. *Courtesy of Fort Monroe's Casemate Museum.*

Aunt Sadie took them. I will never know now how they got there; that's one of the questions I should have asked Granny and did not.

Charles Hickman could not leave the farm to take his family to safety, for to do so would mean abandoning and thus losing his property: "By April 1863, Secretary of War Edwin M. Stanton authorized military governors to take over 'abandoned lands.'"[178] Charles and his son, now twelve, remained on the farm for the duration of the war. The rest of the family prepared to leave home. Once the specific details of the journey were worked out, Uncle Henry and Aunt Sadie were put in charge of the family's welfare, and they all set out for North Carolina. Granny's sister Lelia was born on January 7, 1864, so she was a baby when they left. No stories were told about the trip or the visit with the relatives, and their stay in North Carolina would not have been a long one. Herbert was born in 1866, so the family was reunited soon after the war ended. That journey would have been difficult, to say the least. Uncle Henry and Aunt Sadie must have been extremely capable people to take the family safely over such a long distance during wartime.

9

Coming Home

Rebuilding, New Technology, Boats and Travel and the Old Soldiers' Home

Rebuilding

The Civil War ended officially on April 12, 1865. Lives that had been disrupted during the war would be challenged once again:

> *In four short years, Southern whites had watched their world fall apart. When peace came, they remained uncertain about where and how to start rebuilding their lives—apprehensive, too, about what the Yankees and former slaves might have in mind for them. Former slaves generally rejoiced that they were "free at last," but they, too, were soon overcome with uncertainty. Where would they live? For whom would they work?—Their world, too, had fallen apart.*[179]

The town of Hampton was in ruins, but people still lived there. The Grand Contraband Camp of African Americans was created during the war, using the brick chimneys left standing after the fire and whatever odds and ends of lumber could be scavenged to build shanties for living quarters. This would become the backbone of the free black community in later years.[180] The ex-slaves had remained in Hampton, and their number grew rapidly, as some of the contrabands also chose to stay. After the war, small parcels of land became available for a rather cheap price, and black residents were able to purchase land, one of their first priorities. They bought lots in the west end of Hampton and developed their own housing and business community.[181] Among the businesses going up in the late 1860s was a butcher shop on Queen Street owned by a black man named Walker Hickman.[182] I don't know if he had any relationship with the farm, but he showed the same enterprising spirit as those others who lived there. The town directory of 1896–97 lists Walker H. Hickman as selling meat at his store on Queen Street near Court Street and living on Franklin Street near Lincoln.

As the exiled Hamptonians began to return home that summer of 1865, they had to start over with the basics of life: food and shelter. Property had to be reclaimed and ownership proved. Lumber mills, brickyards and lawyers would have been busy. The town had to be rebuilt almost from scratch after the fire and four years as a Union army encampment. The property owners were able to reclaim their land under the policies laid out in the Reconstruction Plan of President Johnson: "With Congress in recess when the war ended, Johnson took charge of Reconstruction policy. On May 29 [1865] he issued two proclamations; the first granted amnesty to former Confederates who would take an oath of loyalty to the Constitution and the federal laws. Their property was to be restored to them."[183] The rebuilding of homes and businesses on that property, however, took a while, as this newspaper item noted: "Hampton village in the 1870s had more the appearance of a new settlement on the western frontier than that of a two-hundred-year-old Southern town."[184] If there was any advantage to living under Union army occupation for four years, it would be that those citizens had been using Federal currency. Confederate money was completely worthless after the war, and families returning to Hampton from Richmond and other areas controlled by the Confederacy would have had little or no usable money. They stayed with relatives where possible, and traded goods and services to acquire the immediate necessities of life. Rebuilding a proper town would require years of effort.

Returning residents did face a huge challenge: they had to rebuild their homes and businesses, but there were few materials at hand. The Federal government sold the wooden buildings used in the war for a hospital, "and residents salvaged the boards and hardware. Others moved entire buildings and adapted them for housing. One of the wards was put up on North King Street and used as a temporary Methodist church."[185] The Hickman family established a brickyard in the upper part of Pasture Point along the river. J.S. Darling, a newcomer from New York, had a lumber plane mill on Hope Street, and Jacob Heffelfinger started a lumber company in town.[186] There was help available to do the actual building, and men needed work. A number of Hampton men were skilled craftsmen: "The prominent carpenters at the time of Reconstruction were J.W. Brown, an undertaker, Charles Davis Cake, John Wood, W.T. Daougherty, H.D. Owens, and R.S. Hosier."[187]

One example of people "making do with what they had" involved the Wood family. The family home had not burned in the 1861 fire but was torn down later and the lumber used by Union soldiers. When the boys came home after the war, all that remained was "a pile of bricks from the chimney, but John, a carpenter by trade, and Billy, a brick mason, and Sam and George, a pair of handymen, pooled their financial resources—$330 all count—and 'put up a house [for their widowed mother] on the old place,' and, as George wrote in his journal, 'began life again.'"[188]

The reconstruction of the town had a serious setback when a fire broke out in April 1884:

> *The fair little town of Hampton, Virginia, has been visited by a conflagration which has swept away the edge of its business section. The fire broke out at three o'clock yesterday morning, and owing to the high wind spread rapidly. Engines from the Normal School, the Soldiers' Home and Fort Monroe were sent for, and by their united efforts saved half the town from destruction. Thirty buildings, mostly frame, occupied as stores and dwellings, were consumed. The estimated loss is $100,000.*[189]

The fire, although disastrous for the property owners, had a beneficial long-term effect: the temporary wooden structures were replaced sooner than they would have been. Hampton residents refused to give up, and new investments were made by town merchants, both white and black. Francis Anton Schmelz had been the town baker, and when his business was burned with the rest of the town, he went to Richmond for the duration of the war. He wisely invested his Confederate money in real estate and returned to Hampton a wealthy man.[190] His sons had the wherewithal to buy land in town and start literally rebuilding. Henry and George Schmelz, along with many others, began a remarkable era of urban reconstruction in Hampton. For almost thirty years, new buildings went up at a rapid pace. All this activity was possible because of two things: the first banks in town were organized with loans available, and people were determined to make their hometown a success.

To show the enormity of the undertaking, the following time line is offered:

1870s: The Barnes Hotel is founded on South King Street.

1876: The new courthouse opens on North King Street. Part of the burned-out building is used.

1877: Dry goods store is built on the northeast corner of King and Queen Streets (became E.G. Darden's store in 1881).

1879: Warren T. Smith establishes his funeral home on South Court Street.

1881: Henry Schmelz builds a grocery store on the northwest corner of King and Queen Streets; Schmelz Brothers Bank is organized on the second floor. L.H. Sclater now has a drugstore next to the northeast corner of King and Queen.

1885: Post office opens in Henry Schmelz's building on North King Street. Bank of Hampton moves to new building on East Queen Street, south. Henry and George Schmelz build adjoining "brick blocks" on Queen, west of the corner, and put up a new building on King between the post office and their old building on the corner. Sclater & Young have a new store up King, selling "Drugs, Paints, and Farming Implements."

1886: George Schmelz builds a $7,500 brick building on Queen at Wine Street.

1887: A lot is bought on East Queen Street for a Masonic Temple—east was the Bank of Hampton. The Bethel AME Church is built on Lincoln Street.

1888: Lots on Cary Street are offered for sale, and the Baptist Parsonage is built on one. The Methodist church is rebuilt and dedicated. Henry Schmelz builds another "brick block" on South King and a new house on the river by the Queen Street Bridge. Construction of the Queen Street Baptist Church is begun (completed in 1905).

1889: The People's Building & Loan is organized in the basement of the First Baptist Church on North King Street. An office is built on the corner of King and Lincoln. The Pythian Castle, home of the Knights of Pythias Lodge, is built on West Queen. Streetcar line begins service between Hampton and Old Point.

1890: The Queen Street Bridge is rebuilt by the Hampton Manufacturing Company.

1894: The Augusta Hotel is built on East Queen Street.

1896: H.R. Booker sells drugs and hardware in the Sclater building. Schmelz Brothers Bank is in Henry's old store on the northwest corner of King and Queen Streets, rebuilt from the store.

1902: The Barnes Hotel is torn down and replaced by the Kecoughtan Building on South King Street, where the Houston Printing Company is located. The Syms Eaton School is built on Cary Street.

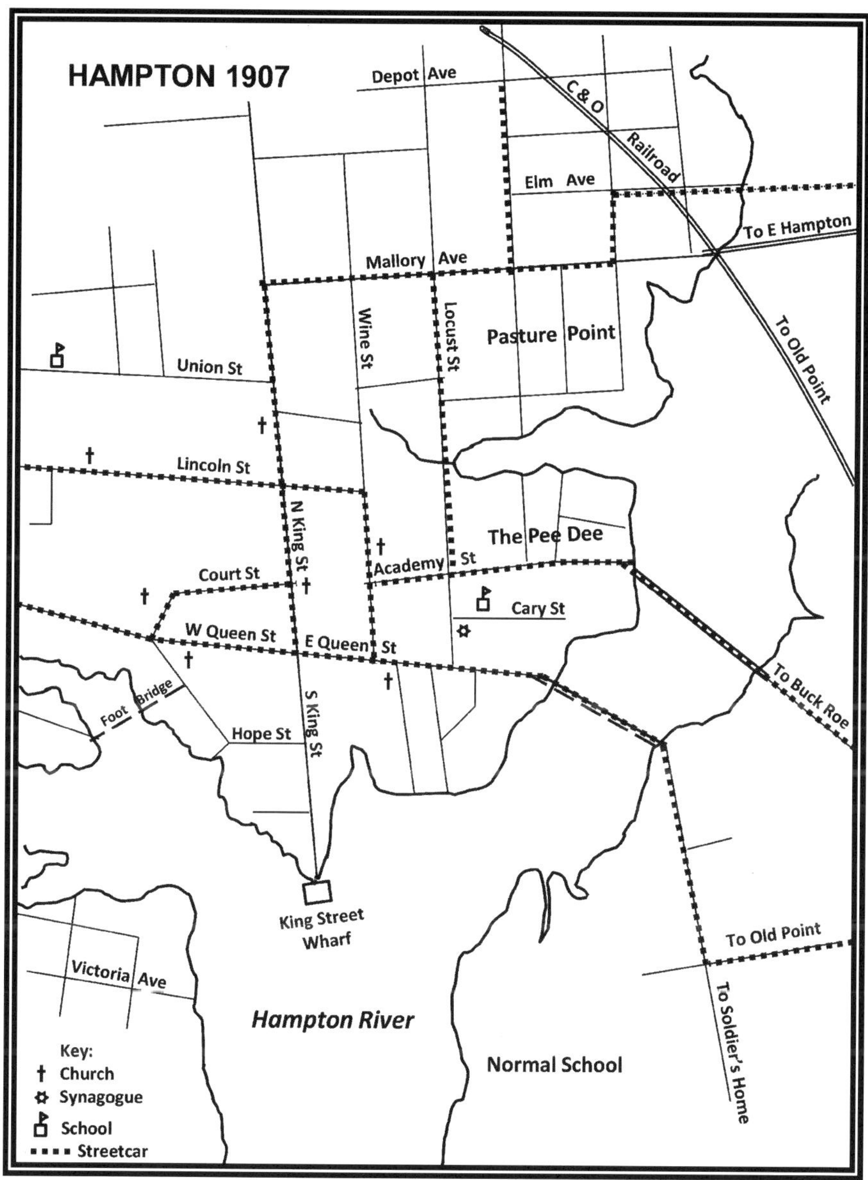

Hampton 1907. This map shows the development of the town of Hampton by 1907 and how the streetcars tied the communities together. Churches and schools share space downtown with shops and banks. The Normal School and the Soldiers' Home are both full participants in the life of the town. *Drawn and revised from Fire Alarm Signal Map of Hampton, 1907, courtesy of Hampton City Library.*

1903: Schmelz Bank is consolidated with the Bank of Hampton, which has a new building on the southeast corner of King and Queen. The First National Bank, organized that year, moves into Schmelz's old place on the northwest corner.
1905: Merchants Bank is built on a narrow lot on the northeast corner of King and Queen Streets.[191]

The cross streets of King and Queen were once again populated with stores and businesses; many Hamptonians have built or rebuilt homes in downtown, especially along the River and South King and South Court Streets; St. John's Episcopal Church was restored; and the white Methodist and Baptist churches were rebuilt. Property was purchased for a synagogue on Locust Street. Black residents were now free to express themselves in their own style of religion, and three African American churches were built in downtown.[192]

In addition to the homes and businesses going up in town, three major industries were developed during this remarkable period of growth: The McMenamin Crab Factory was established in 1879, J.S. Darling's Oyster Plant opened in 1884 and the Hampton Manufacturing Company was founded in 1888. The first two are discussed in the next chapter. The Manufacturing Company is of particular interest as many of the town's leading citizens are listed as stockholders: H.R. and R.M. Booker, A.D. Wallace, J.S. Darling, Dr. Selden, George and Henry Schmelz, C.T. Holtzclaw, H.L. Slater, P.T. Woodfin, H.C. Whiting, J.B. Lake and J.W. Richardson. With such a crowd of supporters, the business was sure to be a success. The plant was built on one and a half acres on North King Street, and S. Hunting Sayre, from Pennsylvania, was hired to run the foundry. Originally, "boilers, machinery, belting, shafting, moulds, etc." were offered for sale:

> *In May, materials to make 10,000 barrels had arrived, the directors having decided to make them also. In August, they advertised that they'd pay ½ cent per pound, 50 cents per 100 lbs, or $10 per ton for up to 1,000,000 lbs of scrap iron—delivered. In October they were advertising "The Hampton Boy, a great plow for truckers"* [truck farmers], *and the Hampton No. 1, No. 3, and No. 5. They also made hitching posts, lawn seats, watering troughs,—and, in 1890, pilings for the Mill Creek and Hampton bridges. By 1896, the Company had become the Hampton branch of Starke's Dixie Plow Works, but Sayre was still the manager.*[193]

Another company investment that offered the town a good return for decades was the *Daily Press* newspaper, which was founded in 1896:

> *The controlling interest in the stock company which bought the paper in 1910 was held by Schmelz Brothers, bankers, who had advanced substantial sums in financing the development and publication of the paper during the first fourteen years of its existence, and whose continued faith in its future probably saved it from bankruptcy.*[194]

The *Daily Press*, although no longer owned by the founding families, is still the local newspaper.

The rebuilding of the town of Hampton included the reestablishment of Old Point Comfort as a resort to attract wealthy visitors to the area. A new Hygeia had appeared as a small restaurant east of the wharf in 1863 and was called the Hygeia Dining Saloon. In 1868, permission was granted by the military to expand the facility into a hotel:

> *In 1876 the hotel passed into the hands of Harrison Phoebus, an astute businessman who had first come to Old Point Comfort as the agent of the Adams Express Company* [after] *the Civil War. Phoebus said, "I will have the best hotel of its kind in the country. And I will let the public know it!" He studied every detail of the hotel business, visiting leading hotels all over the country. "You must compare the best to get the best," he asserted.*[195]

Phoebus was true to his word, and during his lifetime, the hotel flourished. It was also huge. By 1882, the Hygeia was "enlarged with extensions, wings,

The Hygeia Hotel. This is the second Hygeia, and it grew to its enormous proportions by the addition of bits and pieces. As a waterfront hotel, it drew visitors from the north for the healthful sea air in a warmer climate. It occupied the area now known as the Parade Ground at Fort Monroe. *Courtesy of Hampton History Museum, 2009.15.6347.*

and annexes and had reached the stateliness, beauty and dimensions of a palace."[196] It fulfilled the expectations of the town of Hampton by bringing in visitors to spend money and by providing jobs for the townspeople.

In 1865, when Granny's family returned home, the difficult task of rebuilding the town of Hampton and the surrounding area was still ahead. Charles Hickman had held on to his property and kept the farm running with a reduced labor force throughout the war, but by war's end his finances were stretched thin. George Wood, a young boatman, had left Hampton with his family after the town was burned but returned before the war ended. He later wrote in his journal that "all the neighboring farmers had a good trade with milk, vegetables, chickens, and eggs, &c, but none of them seemed to have saved their money, and the merchants got broke after the war."[197] George Wood must not have known that price controls were enacted in the Federally controlled areas of Virginia, and merchants and farmers would not have become rich selling goods and produce to the Union commissary: "Areas [of the South] that escaped the direct ravages of war still suffered from shortages, inflation, high taxes, [and] government impressment of goods and slaves."[198]

Charles Hickman did begin buying property again in 1869. Later, with help from the bank started in 1881 by his new Schmelz sons-in law, he bought 346 acres on Harris Creek, 31 acres on Fox Hill Road and about 80 acres called "North Bend" on the Hampton River near the poorhouse.[199] The farm was again prosperous and well run.

The postwar era brought many changes to Hampton besides the physical ones. At the time when Charles Hickman was buying farmland, his children were moving into town. Mary married the Phillips boy next door, and they lived for a while on his farm before moving to the town of Portsmouth, on the south side of Hampton Roads. Alice never married and lived with a family member wherever she was needed. Probably the most interesting of those experiences was living with Mary's daughter Grace in the governor's mansion in Richmond. Grace's husband was John Garland Pollard, governor of Virginia from 1930 to 1934.

Mattie and Georgie married the Schmelz brothers, Henry and George. Henry built a house on Elm Street in Pasture Point, and the two couples—plus Angelina and Thomas Parramore, newly married—lived there together for several years. One of the advantages of living in town was having neighbors to visit. As their business enterprises grew, Henry and George Schmelz built homes for their individual families on the Hampton River, one on either side of the Queen Street Bridge. It was said that a favorite Sunday afternoon

Along the boulevard—the McMenamin House. When James McMenamin built this house around 1898, there was only one other structure in sight. There is no seawall, and the beach is right out front. This section of the county is just now being developed, and the area west of the house will soon become one of the first golf courses in the state. *Courtesy of Hampton History Museum, CC2013.8.6.*

social event was to "take tea from Schmelz to Schmelz."[200] Fox Hill residents always had close neighbors, and one of the favorite pastimes was visiting and telling stories. One of the older men remembered, "We children would sit listening to our parents and their friends tell something that had happened many years ago, and when the story was getting good they would send us off to bed."[201]

Charles W. Hickman Jr. and his brother, Herbert, left the farm to become the town's grocers. The store, Hickman and Co., was part of the Schmelz property on King Street near Queen. Both brothers built homes in town, in the area called Pasture Point along the Hampton River. Charles was a trustee of Hampton Baptist Church and, in 1885, was instrumental in acquiring land on the Pee Dee Point to build a parsonage.[202]

In 1885, Lelia Hickman married James McMenamin, an Irishman from Massachusetts, one of the Northern "carpetbaggers" who came to the area after the war. He and J.S. Darling, another Northerner from New York, would establish the seafood industry in Hampton. The first house James McMenamin built was on the Hampton River near the Schmelz families. He later built a new home along the shore of Hampton Roads in 1898. This house was the forerunner of the new movement out of town and back to the county. The circle was coming round again.

Angelina Hickman was my grandmother, whom I always called Granny. She married Dr. Thomas H. Parramore, who was born in the upper part of Accomac County on the Eastern Shore. He attended Baltimore Dental College and practiced dentistry in Maryland for several years. He came to Hampton in 1879 and opened his practice of dentistry on King Street near Hope Street. By 1892, he was well established in the community and was on the board of the Dixie Hospital, which was founded in that year. This was the town's first public hospital and was built on the east side of Hampton River near the Normal School.

In 1894, Grandfather bought a lot on Amonate Avenue and Kecotan Avenue in the Wythe district of Elizabeth City County. He built a house and added another lot to the property in 1898.[203] Amonate was renamed Hampton Roads Avenue in the later development of the Armstrong Tract. In October 1905, Aunt Rose and Aunt Louise bought property from the Armstrong Land and Improvement Co., Grandfather built another house and the family moved again. I don't know why the daughters bought the property, but the town clerk knew to whom the land belonged. The deed book has a note written in the margin, "Originals of both deeds delivered to Dr. Parramore on Dec. 22, 1905."[204] The deeds show the property located on Avenue D and Shore Road. These roads are more familiarly known today as Cherokee Road and Chesapeake Avenue. The new house was across the street from the McMenamin property.

The view of Hampton Creek from Rudds Lane, 1905. On a calm winter day, the workboats lie at anchor by the King Street wharf. One man is checking his boat, and the steamboat docked in the background is likely taking on cargo for Norfolk. The waterfront in Hampton has come back to life. *Courtesy of Hampton History Museum, 1952.15.6.*

The Syms-Eaton School/Academy. Hamptons' newest school built after the war was an imposing structure along Cary Street. The half basement gave additional space and didn't flood during exceptional high tides, even though the river was just across the street. The substantial brick building served the town well as a school and later as the school administration building. It was demolished as part of the "urban renewal" craze in the 1980s. *Courtesy of Hampton History Museum, 2009.15.2106.*

Buildings, businesses and houses were now built and occupied. The Elizabeth City County Circuit Court was reestablished in 1870.[205] Children were back in school. The county and town were once again recognizable as a community, although far different from that which existed before the war. If you came home from an extended absence and found your house was just as you left it, you would probably sweep out the dust, wash the curtains, rearrange the furniture and go on living as you had before. The people of Hampton came home and found no house left at all. They could make changes to everything, and they did so. They looked on their accomplishments with a certain sense of pride. When King and Queen Streets were finally paved and "the railway and electric lights came to Hampton in the late 1880's [*sic*],—[Hamptonians] pronounced their village to be one of the 'leading cities in the South.'"[206]

NEW TECHNOLOGY

Streetcars

The "railway" mentioned above was the streetcar line that began service between Hampton and Old Point in 1889. The technology was new and had been invented and then tested by Frank Sprague in Richmond, Virginia, only the year before. Sprague had graduated from the Naval Academy in 1878 but resigned his commission in 1883 to work with Thomas Edison. With this background, he developed the first electric-powered streetcar.

> *After 1888, many cities turned to electric-powered streetcars. To get electricity to the streetcars from the powerhouse where it was generated, an overhead wire was installed over city streets. A streetcar would touch this electric wire with a long pole on its roof. Back at the powerhouse, big steam engines would turn huge generators to produce the electricity needed to operate the streetcars. A new name was soon developed for streetcars powered by electricity; they were called trolley cars.*[207]

The trolley cars ran on steel tracks down the middle of the street. It was relatively easy to put them down in Hampton after the war, because the streets were not yet paved. Electricity came from the coal-fired power plant on Sunset Creek, by Kecoughtan Road. The first streetcar company in Hampton was a corporation consisting of James S. Darling, president, and Henry and George Schmelz, underwriters. That company "merged with two competitors in 1900 to form the widespread Citizens Railway, Light and Power Company. The same company owned Buckroe Beach, which was convenient since the trolley company made it easy for visitors to get to the seaside resort. The company saw to it that

> *extra-heavy trolley rails were laid at Buckroe so that Chesapeake & Ohio excursion trains from Richmond could deliver their passengers next door to the picnic pavilion. Freight trolleys as well as passenger trolleys served the Peninsula in those early days. Francis Schmelz* [father of Henry and George] *operated a bakery and confectionery on Queen Street in Hampton and used the morning trolley service to send thousands of pastries each workday to the Newport News Shipyard to be sold by vendors outside the gates at lunchtime.*[208]

Queen Street looking east, 1910. Most of the wooden buildings have been replaced with brick structures, and the trolley tracks have been laid down the middle of the street, leaving little room for the horse and buggy on the right. Awnings give some shade to the storefronts and the shoppers in the summer weather. *Courtesy of Hampton History Museum, 0376.01.*

When the Queen Street Bridge was repaired in 1890, special provisions were made for the streetcars. "J.S. Darling offered to pay $9,000 of the cost if guaranteed right of way for his Electric Railway...By November, tongers were taking up oysters in the way of the new bridge. Nine feet of the bridge was for the railway, twenty for the driveway, and six for pedestrians."[209] The pedestrians would likely be going between the Soldiers' Home, the Normal School and the Town of Hampton. Also, Henry and George Schmelz lived on either side of the Hampton River by the bridge, so there must have been a lot of foot traffic.

At night, the trolley cars would be lined up in the car barns on the aptly named Electric Avenue, about a mile north of Granny's house. There were at one time sixty streetcars in use, and everybody rode them. Fox Hill women had two grocery stores in the village in which to shop, but now and then, something was needed from Hampton. They used to walk there and back, but with the advent of the streetcar, they walked the shorter distance to Buckroe and rode the trolley into town.[210] A Fox Hill woman worked for the telephone company in Hampton. Every day she rode her bicycle halfway and then took the streetcar.[211] The outlying areas in the west end of the county, such as the Boulevard and Wythe, began to be developed as residential property since one could get to work in town or to school by riding the streetcar. Dr. Parramore rode the trolley every day to his dentistry office on King Street in downtown. The Schmelz brothers were both bankers and divided the business between them. Henry was president of the Hampton Bank, and George was president of the Schmelz Brothers Bank on Washington Avenue in downtown Newport News. George was another daily commuter on the streetcar from Hampton. There are many memories of riding the streetcar that could be explored, but here are two:. Parke Rouse, a writer for the *Daily Press* newspaper, remembered, "Over the motor man's head a sign warned: 'Please do not speak to the motor man. His duties require all of his attention.'"[212] I remember an even more important sign that read, "No Expectorating." We had to know some pretty big words when I was little.

Boats and Travel

The easiest way to get around the Peninsula has always been by boat, from the log canoes of the Kicotan Indians to the modern steamboat developed in 1809. After the Civil War, when the area's roads were in terrible shape, people used all kinds of water transport, from the sailing log canoes of the watermen to the family sailboat or rowboat and the large Bay Line Steamboats that carried passengers to neighboring towns and up the Chesapeake Bay to Washington and Baltimore. Steamboat travel for civilians was prohibited during the war, but service picked up again soon afterward. In a visitors' guide to the Hampton area written in 1883, the author gave information about how to travel by boat. The trip across the harbor to the city of Norfolk, a distance of sixteen miles, took one hour by steamer. Four different steamboats carried passengers across, starting at seven o'clock in the morning, and the return trips started at three o'clock in the afternoon. The cost was fifty cents one way or seventy-five cents round trip. To visit the Eastern Shore or Matthews County, you could sail in style:

> *The steamer* Northampton *leaves Old Point Comfort on Monday, Wednesday, and Friday, at 8.30 a.m., for Cherrystone, on the eastern shore of Virginia—famous for its oysters, which are accounted among the finest*

The steamer *Old Point Comfort*, circa 1905. The steamboat shown here is typical of those plying the harbor and the bay across to the Eastern Shore and up to Matthews County. The *Old Point Comfort* looks clean and comfortable, and its speed was sufficient to get you to your destination in a timely fashion with time to enjoy the view. *Courtesy of Library of Congress, Prints & Photographs Division, Detroit Publishing Company Collection, LC-D4-21849.*

The government dock, Old Point Comfort, Virginia. Cargo waiting to be loaded on board a steamer is neatly stacked and organized on the wharf, while what appears to be a group of passengers wait at the edge of the depot building. The imposing Chamberlin Hotel fills the background in this picture from circa 1905. *Library of Congress, Prints & Photographs Division, Detroit Publishing Company Collection, LC-D4-33820.*

Oyster boats (Chesapeake Bay log canoes) identified as the J.S. Darling & Co.'s fleet. The graceful boats shown here are of different sizes and have subtle differences in shape. Each was immediately identified by its owner and, in spite of its delicate appearance, was a true workboat. The Hampton waterfront is in the background. *Courtesy of Hampton History Museum, 2009.15.2387.*

> *in the United States—returning at 2 p.m.; on Tuesday, Thursday, and Saturday, at 8.30 a.m., for Matthews and Ware River, returning at 4 p.m. These steamers are first class in all their appointments, and the ride across Chesapeake Bay and Hampton Roads is delightful.*[213]

That ticket would cost you one dollar round trip.

During the summer, James River Steamers would take you to Richmond every other day. You could get to Washington or Baltimore directly by the Bay Line Steamers every day and to New York on the Old Dominion Line from Norfolk on Monday through Thursday and Saturday.[214] From those large cities, you could catch a train to wherever else you wanted to go. Hampton was literally connected to the whole country through its network of steamboats.

Men who came to the area as ship's carpenters established an industry that became well known on the entire Peninsula:

> *The boatbuilders of bygone days were truly great craftsmen. These men never had blueprints to construct their boats. The boatman's eye was his plans and blueprints—They took great pride in their work. These boatbuilders had certain lines that could be recognized in each boat they built. If a boat passed you in the Bay or was tied up at a dock, someone would say, "There is a so-and-so built boat."*[215]

Boats were, of course, essential in the waterman's trade, and most of them were made locally. In the early 1800s, there were shipbuilders in Hampton on the town waterfront, and in Fox Hill, men were building schooners in small shipyards on Harris Creek, Back River and Wallace Creek.[216] These boatyards also made the log canoes used by the men bringing in both crabs and oysters. The canoes were built the old-fashioned way: "Five hefty logs, an old broad ax, a foot adz, a strong back, and a knowledge of Chesapeake Bay boatbuilding that spans three hundred years, that's what it takes to build a Chesapeake Bay log canoe."[217] Actually, a log canoe can be made from one, three, five, seven or even nine logs, but the five-log boat is the traditional one.[218] The canoe is very stable, which is essential for its use by watermen, especially those tonging for oysters: "Oystermen stand on the washboards of a boat as they work [the long-handled tongs]. They must have a strong platform...The washboard had to be wide enough so a man's feet could fit between the coaming [collar board] and the toe rail. If a man had big feet, he'd order a wider washboard."[219]

The canoes are carved out of logs from pine trees, which grow straight and tall, and the soft wood makes it easier to chop out the hull. The bottom log is the keel log, the next two are called garboard logs and the top two are the bilge logs. These logs are then "all shaped with a broad ax, a foot adz, and a handsaw."[220] After shaping, the logs are put together today with bolts, but "way back they used pins or 'trunnels' of locust wood."[221] The word "trunnel" is a corruption of the words "tree nail" and has acquired a life of its own in the boatman's vocabulary.[222] Once the hull is fastened together, "the inside has to be chopped out and smoothed down."[223] A log canoe has pointed "deadrise" ends, and these are shaped next. A further step is needed here to raise the sides to the desired height. This is done "by installing 'raising' wood along the top edge of the bilge logs."[224] The centerboard well is cut through the keel log, and the boat is trimmed out. On this particular canoe, "the mast is twenty-six feet long and the boom is thirteen feet long. Both are made from white cedar. 'It was always a rule of thumb that the length of the mast and the length of the keel be the

Log canoe construction process: (1) Five pine trees were cut to length, and the initial shaping of a log with hand tools was begun. The bottom, or center log, is the keel; the next two are the garboards; and the top two are the bilge logs. *Courtesy of Hampton History Museum, 2008.63.9.*

(2) The outside logs are shaped alongside the keel. These logs can have a slight bend to them since they will be carved that way. *Courtesy of Hampton History Museum, 2008.63.11.*

(3) All five logs are roughly shaped and fastened together to form the hull of a log canoe. *Courtesy of Hampton History Museum, 2008.63.12.*

(4) The keel has taken shape, and the form of the canoe is apparent. *Courtesy of Hampton History Museum, 2008.63.14.*

(5) The inside of the canoe has been chopped out and smoothed with hand tools. The "rising" boards are now being put in place. *Courtesy of Hampton History Museum, 2008.63.15.*

(6) The nearly completed Chesapeake Bay log canoe is a beautiful boat. This one is twenty-six feet long, and with the addition of its mast and a coat of paint, it will be ready to sail. *Courtesy of Hampton History Museum, 2008.63.18.*

same.'"[225] The mast is five inches in diameter, tapering to two and three-quarters inches at the top. These proportions make the log canoe a beautiful sailing boat. With several men helping with the chopping and shaping, a boat took about nine months to build.[226]

A special kind of boat was built in Fox Hill and the Buckroe area for use in pound-net fishing. This was a scow-type boat "designed to be put out through the surf and pulled back up on the beach at the end of the day's work."[227] Sails and oars powered the early boats, which were "34 feet long for Bay use, with a 6 foot beam and a depth of 3 feet."[228]

Wooden boats kept in the salt water around the Peninsula needed special care to keep them in good shape. Once a year, the boat would be hauled out of the water and its bottom inspected. Barnacles had to be scraped off, caulking replaced and a new coat of red marine paint put on. Small boats could be worked on at home, but the large ones were taken to a marine railway for maintenance. There were a number of those available, such as J.H. Gosline's on the west side of Hampton River and J.S. Darling's in town.[229] They were busy, especially in the spring, with many customers needing their services. Hampton was a harbor town.

Old Soldiers' Home

The National Home for Disabled Volunteer Soldiers was established by an act of Congress on March 3, 1865. The local, or Southern Branch, as it was officially known, came into being in 1870 when "the old Chesapeake Female College, which had been used as a hospital during the war, was purchased for the government together with the forty acres of land owned by General B.F. Butler for $50,000."[230] The Civil War hospital here had been "the great receiving place for sick and wounded soldiers of the Federal army in Virginia,"[231] and thus the site was appropriate for the location of a home where some of those aging Union veterans could finish out their lives in comfort and with excellent care. As one of the former soldiers described it:

> *We are not inmates, but members, showing that we are entitled by right of claim to all the U.S. Government can do for us in our old age, as a slight recompense in part for what we accomplished in our youth in saving our Country from dissolution and ruin. We are therefore not mendicants or paupers, but OLD SOLDIERS and SAIOLORS, who sacrificed our health and the opportunity, had we stayed at home, of accumulating wealth.*[232]

The National Soldiers' Home, Hampton, circa 1902. The size of the main building can easily be seen in this picture. The many floors with verandas all face the water, giving great views of the harbor. The grounds are beautifully kept, and there is a walkway all along the river. *Courtesy of Library of Congress, Prints & Photographs Division, Detroit Publishing Company Collection, LC-D4-14187.*

The Old Soldiers' Home, as it came to be known, was (and still is) located along the east side of the Hampton River, between the two creeks opposite Blackbeard's Point. The waterfront provides not only a beautiful view but also a lively scene of activity to enjoy, especially if the observer is somewhat limited in his mobility. Forty-three more acres and many buildings were added to the original home. It was built to house about 350, but by 1883, there were 1,500 members. One of the residents described the many advantages to be found in the home: "As far as possible, everything necessary to make the place comfortable and attractive to the members has been done."[233] In the main building, where the men are housed, everything is neat and in order, as befits a military establishment. Other amenities are included, as well: "We find wash-rooms, bath-rooms, and other conveniences on every floor, while an elevator is running at all times for the accommodation of those veterans who are afflicted or too old to walk up and down the stairway."[234] On the very top floor, there was a piazza along the entire front of the building, from which one could see the harbor.

In Ward Memorial Hall, sixteen tables are laid and ready for one thousand men to have their next meal. "It takes over 1,000 lbs. of beef at one meal, and about 1,000 loaves of bread daily. The latter is all baked on the place. The bill of fare changes daily and varies with the seasons:

SOLDIERS' HOME BILL OF FARE FOR ONE DAY[235]

Breakfast	**Dinner**	**Supper**
Ham	Roast Beef	Stewed Prunes
Bread	Bread	Bread
Potatoes	Butter	Butter
Eggs	Potatoes	Cheese
Butter	Rice Pudding	Tea
Coffee	Coffee	

For entertainment, there was a billiard room; a fully stocked library, with 146 newspapers and 115 magazines; and a theater that seated 915 members. The conservatory held beautiful plants and flowers. For exercise, there was a boardwalk along the entire waterfront, and opportunities were available for boating, fishing and "salt water bathing [from] the dock at the mouth of the creek."[236] A hospital on the grounds treated about eighty-five patients daily.

Of particular interest to the citizens of Hampton were the steam fire department, which answered the call to the town in the 1884 fire, and the excellent military band at the home. Everyone was invited to its concerts held every afternoon, except Sundays, from three to four o'clock. The home also provided employment for many local men and women. Doctors, nurses, cooks, waiters, cleaners, gardeners and farmers all could find work there. From December 1884 to November 1891, the *Soldiers' Home Bulletin* was the unofficial newspaper of Hampton.[237] As judged by the experience of the local members and their neighbors in town, the National Soldiers' Home was a good investment by the U.S. government.

10

The Seafood Industry

Crabs and Oysters

Various kinds of seafood have been caught and eaten in the area since there have been people here to enjoy it. The readily available food source was an important criterion in determining to settle here in the first place. Until the 1880s, the harvesting of seafood was largely done on a small-scale basis, with individuals investing in boats and selling their harvest locally. One exception to this took place on the aptly named Factory Point strip of land separating the Chesapeake Bay and the mouth of Back River:

> *There once was a fish factory there in the middle and late 1800s. Sailing schooners brought loads of menhaden or "bunker fish" to the factory. The fish were cooked in large kettles and spread on wooden platforms or drying racks. They were built above the sand and here the sun and wind dried the cooked fish. Oil from the drying fish drained into a trough built around the edge of the platforms. The oil was barreled up and sold to paint manufacturers and for other purposes, like medicines. The rest of the fish dried like paper. This was bagged and loaded aboard schooners to be shipped up the bay for farmers to use for fertilizer. Those who remember the factory in operation said that when the wind was blowing from the north and east, the fumes were terrible.*[238]

In post–Civil War Hampton, a great many things changed, including the whole range of fishing industries. James McMenamin, the Irishman from Massachusetts, had been in Norfolk (across the Hampton Roads) developing

Menhaden fishing, circa 1897. The men in the boats are bringing in a net filled with menhaden, or mossbunkers. The fish were used for their oil and as fertilizer. Menhaden oil was cheaper than whale oil and easier to come by. *Courtesy of Library of Congress LC-USZ-71305.*

a method of processing crabs so that they could be shipped around the country. In 1879, he moved to Hampton, where the crabbing industry was flourishing, and established McMenamin Crab Factory on the Hampton River at the foot of Victoria Avenue opposite the Normal School. The business was extremely successful, with a fleet of fifty to sixty boats bringing in crabs every day. By 1907, the company was processing and selling crabmeat not only across the country but also to China, the Philippines, India, South Africa, Cuba, Mexico, Alaska and South America:[239] "His process won prizes in Berlin, London, and Paris…[and] at the height of his business, McMenamin grossed $5 million per year. Robert Peary carried tins of McMenamin crabmeat to the North Pole."[240] Other crab factories were built along the creeks, and the area became so well known for its crabs that Hampton is called "Crab Town." The high school sports teams are known to this day as the "Hampton Crabbers."

A general understanding of a crab's life can be gained through knowing the names given to the various stages of the adult crab. Crabs grow by shedding their hard shells and immediately expanding. The new, soft shell is fully developed underneath the old, hard one. The hard shell begins to separate along the back edge, and the crab literally backs out, leaving its old shell, or "shed," behind. This process is also called "moulting." The "hard crab" or "jimmy" is the stage at which the familiar crab meat is taken. The "peeler" is the early getting-ready-to-shed stage, and the "buster" is about to back out. The "soft crab" is also eaten and greatly enjoyed. Soft crabs are caught by walking along the shallow water when the tide is going out and looking

McMenamin's crab fleet and factory in Hampton River, circa 1900. The men are probably preparing the trotlines they will work during the day. Eel was the preferred bait because it was cheap and easy to come by. The sailboat coming into the river is a reminder of the beauty that was once seen daily on the Hampton waterfront. *Courtesy of Hampton History Museum, 1997.3.162.*

McMenamin & Company sign, circa 1910. The Chesapeake Bay blue crab is the subject here in a local artist's work. The oil painting is almost four feet across and once hung in the office of the McMenamin & Company crab factory along the Hampton River. It had been cut from its frame and rolled up after the company was sold. After many years, it was rediscovered and restored. Today, it beautifully represents "Crab Town" and now has a home in the Hampton History Museum. *Courtesy of Hampton History Museum,* 2013.19.1.

in the seaweed and other sheltered places. When it is in the soft stage, the crab is completely defenseless and has to hide from its predators, including other crabs. When it is found, the crab is carefully scooped in a hand net and put in a basket lined with seaweed to keep it fresh. "Peelers" are put in

Trotline crabbing, circa 1890s. The waterman here is tending his trotline. He pulled the boat along the line and dipped the crabs feeding on the bait into his net. The crabs then went into the barrel seen behind him and would be taken at the end of the day to the McMenamin & Company crab factory. *Courtesy of Hampton History Museum, CC2013.8.1.*

shedding floats and checked regularly to remove the soft crabs. Between the soft and back-to-hard stage is what the Virginia Institute of Marine Science calls "buckram" crabs. We always called them "papershells," and we hated to catch one because it was neither hard nor soft, and we let it go. There are male and female crabs, which can be distinguished by the shape of the abdomen, or "apron"; the male's is narrow at the top, and the female's is more rounded. I have heard them described as the Washington Monument and the Capitol dome. The female carries its eggs outside the apron in an orange, sponge-like mass and therefore is called a "sponge crab."

When the weather starts to get cold, the hard crabs head out to deep water, which will not freeze. From April 1 to December 1, crabs are back in shallower water, and the crabbers head out in their log canoes to tend the trotlines: "This gear includes a ground line, baited with tripe or salted eel, which is run over a roller that extends from the side of the boat. The crabs holding on to the bait are brought to the surface."[241] They are then shaken off into a hand net beside the boat. Some trotlines could be "as long as 1,500 feet, dangling crab bait every foot or so."[242]

The trotline crabbing process "is one of the oldest methods used to harvest Chesapeake blue cabs."[243] The ubiquitous chicken wire "crab pot" of today's waterfront is a more modern invention. Benjamin F. Lewis created his first wire crab pot in 1928: "He revised the pot in 1938 and received a second patent on his invention that year. The 1938 crab pot is almost identical to the pots that are used today all over the world."[244]

After being out on the water all day, the watermen took their catch to the crab factories, where the crabs were steamed, picked by hand and the meat processed for canning. The crabber's catch was measured by the barrel: "One barrel of crabs will average about twelve pounds of meat, about one ounce per crab."[245] The crab pickers were traditionally black women, who could be identified by their white caps and aprons.

Crabs are not only good to eat but also good for you: "Crabs are a highly nutritious food. White crab meat is as rich or richer in calcium, magnesium, phosphorus, iron and copper than most seafoods. It contains about six times as much iodine as milk and over forty times as much as beef. Crabs are a rich source of vitamins, especially vitamins A, B_1 and C."[246]

As the town of Hampton recovered from the physical devastation of the Civil War, the crab and oyster industries were responsible for a large portion of the economic recovery of the area: "Federal statistics show that in 1904 Virginia produced 7,612,299 bushels of oysters…[and] in 1904 our crab production was 10,356,052 pounds."[247] Furthermore, "the commercial

Crab pickers at S.S. Coston & Co., 1907. The women picking crabs here are dressed in the traditional white gown and cap. Each seems to have adopted her own method of work; some are seated while others stand. Regardless of the method, there is a great deal of crabmeat ready for packing. *Courtesy of Hampton History Museum, 2009.15.2023.*

hard crab industry of Virginia is located in the lower waters of the Chesapeake Bay [and] Hampton is the center of this industry."[248] The sale of all this seafood brought money into the whole town. Watermen were black as well as white, so the larger community participated in wage-earning employment. The crab shells were put to good use as fertilizer, and the fertilizer plant in Hampton smelled just as much as the menhaden fish plant did in Grand View.

The oyster industry was also thriving in Hampton after the war. The other Northerner who came South and founded a seafood industry was James Sands Darling. He was born in New York City, worked on an aunt's farm and then was sent to Long Island to his brother's shipway to learn a trade. By the end of the Civil War, he was ready for a change and selected Virginia and the burned-over town of Hampton as the place for a new start. In 1866, he settled his wife and infant son in a house on King Street, bought a sawmill and a gristmill in town and brought a shipload of lumber down to build houses.[249] He later found his real calling in the oyster business. In 1882, when the Hampton Bar was opened for leasing, Darling rented acreage and started oyster planting.[250] His business became so successful that the landscape of

Oyster pile, Hampton, between 1900 and 1920. This is the Hampton "pyramid" of oyster shells by the J.S. Darling oyster house. It could be seen from anywhere in town and represented the incomes of many residents. *Courtesy of Library of Congress, Prints & Photographs Division, Detroit Publishing Company Collection, LC-D4-71087.*

Hampton's waterfront became noted for the four-story pyramid of oyster shells discarded by the shuckers.

Virginia's policy regarding the taking of seafood, and especially oysters, has been guided by the "ancient belief that all things in and under the water should be free to all."[251] The state required only that the watermen buy a license for a nominal fee: "For more than a century Virginia has followed the policy of holding in trust for the benefit of the people of this state, the natural oyster beds."[252] Where oysters grow naturally has been a matter of dispute over the years. To answer this question, in 1892 "a survey was made of the tidewater area by J.B. Baylor, of the United States coast and geodetic survey, for the purpose of preserving and setting aside within definite limits, the natural producing bottoms of the state for the benefit of all of the citizens of the state."[253] Two categories were established: 1) within the Baylor survey, or "natural rock" and 2) outside the Baylor survey, where oysters have to be cultivated. The second category sets aside acreage that "may be leased to any resident of the state who desires to use it for oyster culture."[254] In this now defined territory, Darling and others planted oysters following the process "started in France about 1853, when M. de Bon demonstrated that 'spat,' or oyster spawn, would attach on various objects planted in the water, such as wood, stones and shells."[255] These oysters take about two to five years to reach maturity.

The individual oystermen work the natural rock, which "consists largely of beds of old oysters and oyster shells, which provide an excellent foundation for the baby oyster to fasten upon."[256] The men, called "tongers," work standing in a boat wielding tongs, or "long paired sticks with rake-like contrivances on their ends, operated like shears…[T]o work them backwards and forwards, breaking the oysters from their holdings, is a task requiring both strength and skill."[257] At this point, the "culling" takes place, which "means that all empty shells and all oysters under three inches in length are separated from the full-grown and are thrown back."[258] Each man works in his own boat, and at the end of the day "takes his catch to a larger boat commonly called the 'buy boat' with which he bargains for the sale of his catch."[259] A tonger "gets ten bushels on an average day,"[260] and weather conditions often keep him off the water. Just as the crabbers had a season of the year in which to work, the oystermen traditionally worked their season in the months that have an *r* in the name, i.e., September through April.

Once the oysters are harvested, they are taken to shucking houses along the creeks and the Hampton waterfront. There the "shuckers," mostly black men, exhibit their skill: "On their left hand they wear a heavy mitten, with which they hold the oyster on a small block, while with their right hand they insert between the shells a knife, cut the muscle and then extract the meat…Per day, a shucker will handle ten or twelve gallons of oysters."[261] The largest, fattest ones, called "counts," are the premium quality, followed by "selects" and "standards." "The oysters, after being washed, are poured

Men tonging oysters from Chesapeake Bay log canoes, circa 1900. These men would be working a leased oyster ground, probably J.S. Darling's. All the boats are log canoes with their sails furled and out of the way for the day's work. *Courtesy of Hampton History Museum, 2013.9.1.*

Buy boat. This large boat loaded with the product of the oystermen's workday is beautiful in spite of its rough appearance. It is headed into Hampton River and the oyster house, probably J.S. Darling's. *Courtesy of Hampton History Museum, 2013.9.8.*

into regulation cans in which they are shipped in iced tubs," principally to Baltimore, Philadelphia, New York and Chicago.[262]

Oyster shells have always been put to good use as road or walkway material, which also provided work for local men. The main road

Oyster shuckers. The men are working on the dock at J.S. Darling's, shucking oysters to be packed and shipped to market. On this sunny day, the outdoor work is not unpleasant, and many oysters are being prepared. *Courtesy of Hampton History Museum, 2013.9.2.*

through Fox Hill was once made with loose oyster shells, as the following account records:

> *A man was appointed by the county government as overseer of the roads. His job was to keep the road passable. This meant filling in the holes with shells which he bought from local oystermen. He also hired local residents to repair the road. The figures below are from the records of the Elizabeth City County Board of Supervisors monthly meeting in 1905. These funds were paid to men of Fox Hill who lived in the Chesapeake District.*
> *W.F. Wallace—1200 Bushs. shells $36.00*
> *W.F. Lewis—300 Bushs. shells $9.00*
> *R.E. Johnson—500 Bushs. shells $15.00*
> *In August that year, Jas. Routten was paid $1.75 for two days work.*[263]

One of the early roads leading out of Hampton to the west of the county was made of oyster shells and is called Shell Road to this day.

The oyster shells are composed of around 95 percent calcium carbonate ($CaCO_3$). This provides a raw material for producing lime (CaO) by a high-temperature burning process. This occurs by way of the reaction $CaCO_3$ + heat → CaO + CO_2. At this point, the lime (CaO) can be used along with fertilizer to condition, or sweeten, acidic soil. To make mortar, the lime is slaked in water to produce calcium hydroxide ($Ca(OH)_2$) and follows the reaction $CaO + H_2O \rightarrow Ca(OH)_2$.[264] The calcium hydroxide is mixed with sand and water, used in the building process and allowed to cure. It was reported that oyster shells were "burned to supply lime in mortar being used as late as 1914 in the Elks Hall on S. King Street."[265]

The seafood industry provided employment for a great many Hamptonians, from building and maintaining the boats to the harvesting and processing of the crabs and oysters, the shipping of the final product and the conversion of the waste products into usable commodities. The organization of all this industry came with the restoration of the town after the war, and the opportunity to start over with something new. Northern entrepreneurs came South to make a living but stayed to live their lives as part of the community. James McMenamin married Granny's sister Lelia and thus became my great-uncle.

11

Public Schools Revisited, the Black Community and the Hampton Normal and Agricultural Institute

By the end of the Civil War, there were around twenty-five thousand black refugees living in settlements in or near Hampton, and many of them had been there for much of the war. That many people, most of them new to the area, needed a great deal of help: "The majority of blacks spent their first years of freedom in wretched poverty, confined to inadequate housing in refugee camps, and barely able to subsist on irregular government wages or scanty government rations."[266] Help did come from Northern missionaries:

> *The American Missionary Association was the first Northern benevolent organization to send aid to Southern contrabands...The Association was already fifteen years old by 1861 and, from its inception, had been dedicated to "preaching the Gospel free from all complicity with slavery and caste." Though officially a nonsectarian evangelical society, the Association was closely allied with the Congregational and Presbyterian Churches; it was this form of evangelical Christianity that it sought to spread to the South. Its leadership had strong ties to the abolitionist movement and was deeply committed to the uplift of the black man, whether slave or free.*[267]

The American "slave codes" laid down very specifically what could and could not be done by and to slaves; for example, slaves could not own property. One of the more specific prohibitions had to do with education. Virginia law, in the Revised Code of 1819, stated, "All meetings or assemblages of slaves, or free negroes or mulattoes mixing and associating with such slaves at any meeting house, &c., in the night; or at any school or schools for teaching them reading or writing, either in the day or night, under whatsoever pretext, shall be deemed and considered an unlawful assembly."[268] The punishment for such an offense could be "at the discretion of any justice of the peace, not exceeding twenty lashes."[269]

The law was applied unevenly throughout the state, and when the missionaries arrived in Hampton in September 1861, black residents were already being taught to read by Mary Peake. She was the daughter of a Frenchman and a mulatto woman, and her father had paid for her to be educated.[270] She had established her school in Brown Cottage, next to the abandoned Chesapeake Female Seminary between Hampton and Fort Monroe. At that time, there were forty-nine pupils, with more expected.[271] Mary and her husband, Thomas, were leaders in the free black community before the war and took their responsibilities seriously:

> *Mary did not allow her education to go to waste. She taught reading to free blacks and slaves alike. Teaching slaves was, of course, against Virginia law, but, like so much else in ante-bellum Hampton, it went unchallenged by white residents so long as it was done discretely and caused no problems. Mrs. Peake continued her school openly after the war began and was one of the first teachers of ex-slaves in the Civil War South.*[272]

The missionaries had often acted as liaisons between the contraband and the Union army, and this was especially true in regard to schools. By December 1861, the AMA (American Missionary Association) had helped start three more schools, in addition to the one taught by Mary Peake. All these early classes were taught by local African Americans. By the end of 1863, the schools were established institutions and were taught mainly by missionaries: "The goal was to provide each student with a 'good English education' and to make each a 'good Christian'…The missionaries interspersed education with Union politics; they meant to teach freedom as well as the 'three Rs.'"[273] Adults as well as children benefitted from the missionaries' efforts: "A large number of 'Union Primers' [were distributed] among the blacks, and…working men took every moment of leisure to study their books, and teach each other to read."[274]

The interest in education and the ability of black students to learn so readily surprised the AMA teachers: "To some degree, however, they were victims of their own abolitionist propaganda. In the effort to promote antislavery sentiment in the North, the abolitionists may have overdrawn the brutalizing effects of bondage upon black people, at least upon those who lived in places like Hampton."[275] The most successful of the missionary schools met in the renovated Hampton courthouse. So many contraband enrolled that the 250 students had to be divided into a lower and an upper level. The upper-level students were taught "multiplication, division, penmanship, and elementary reading...Major problems in all the schools were discipline and the transient population. The freed children tended to be unruly, and often order could be maintained only through generous applications of the rod."[276]

Thanks to the efforts of the missionaries, schools for the black community continued throughout the war: "During the years of war in Hampton, the American Missionary Association workers achieved spectacular success in educating freedmen." Their efforts in inculcating proper religious beliefs and moral behavior, however, were seen by the workers themselves as disappointing:

> *The missionaries came to Hampton with the expectation that the blacks were different from themselves and in great need of assistance, which they would willingly provide. They only gradually came to understand that, in aiding black development, they meant for the blacks to develop along the same lines as themselves in both religious and social behavior. That the blacks might not wish to do so surprised and dismayed them.*[277]

The schools that they had established, however, remained as a testament to their efforts, and in 1865, there were six missionary schools operating in Hampton and Elizabeth City County. After the war, the "graded school for freedmen [in the old courthouse] was transferred to the Lincoln School, which had been built of old hospital wards."[278] The training that the missionaries brought to the black children thus continued as the county picked up the responsibility for their education.

Five years after the Civil War, public schools were starting to reappear across the state of Virginia. The first annual Virginia School Report of 1871 illustrated the newness of the system: county superintendents had just been appointed, a census of the school population was completed, the number and location of schools was determined, teachers were examined and hired and "the first schools were opened about the middle of November [1870]."[279]

The major new component of the school system was seen in the classrooms and in the schoolyards. Virginia's public schools were now educating the black population. The schools were separate for each race, but the state superintendent pointed out that "the difference in the relative number of white and colored schools was accidental...[the state tried to] avoid everything that would even present the appearance of unfairness."[280] The main concern across the state was the need for funds to support this education that was being offered free to all children. The idea that "a specific tax of one mill in the dollar...on the assessed value of the property of the State should be levied to meet this demand [the cost of supporting the Public Free Schools of the State] was proposed by the legislature."[281] Where this idea was put to a local vote, the people approved; school was a necessity.

Here are some statistics of the early years of Virginia's postwar public school system. Only about half of the counties had been able to open their schools at the beginning of the school year in 1870. It was encouraging to note that "a large proportion of these schools have heretofore existed as private schools, which, by the concurrence of those concerned, have now been adopted into the State system, and made free to all." By the end of the school year, "the number of schools had increased to more than 2,000, with about 130,000 pupils and more than 3,000 teachers."[282] A few more statistics are of interest; teachers received about $30 a month as salary; the length of the school year was five months; and there was a "difficulty in procuring qualified teachers for the colored schools."[283] The Normal School at Hampton would soon meet that need.

Elizabeth City County, which included the town of Hampton, had eleven schools open in 1871, eight white (one of which was the Hickman School) and three black. In addition, there were three white and three black private schools, with 50 white children and 85 black children enrolled.[284] The county school population (between five and twenty-one years of age) included 340 white males, 314 white females, 810 black males and 810 black females. Of that population, 372 white children and 277 black children were enrolled in school. The average attendance for white children was 230 while that of black children was 174. Nine children were furnished with schoolbooks at public expense. Illiteracy in the county of people aged ten and over included 2,308 who could not read and 3,055 who could not write.[285] The free public schools had arrived just in time.

Six years later, there was marked improvement. One goal of the state superintendent was to "lengthen the school term from five months to nine or ten months."[286] He recognized that this was a problem because some parents were "compelled to use the labor of their children during a large part of the year."[287] Elizabeth City County in 1877 had an enrollment of 419 white children, or 55 percent of the white school population, and 875 black children, or 51 percent of the black school population. The average monthly attendance was 357 white students and 732 black students. Fifty children were supplied with textbooks at public expense. The good news was that more children were in school; the bad news was that many children were not. The Butler School on the Normal School property and the Lincoln School downtown had the largest enrollment of black children, and the Little England Chapel may have been used as a day school. Samuel Chapman Armstrong, in his report of the Hampton Normal School for the year 1877, declared, "The hard times and the scarcity of money in the South, contrary to expectation, have not caused a diminished attendance this year…the school may hope to graduate annually from fifty to sixty trained teachers."[288] Those graduates would teach in the black schools across the South, but many of the local alumni would teach in Hampton. That was unqualified good news.

THE BLACK COMMUNITY

At the close of the Civil War, the black community in Hampton was still evolving. The changes actually began several years earlier: "With each passing day after the spring of 1862, Hampton's original contraband were becoming more and more of a minority in their own black community. By the first wartime census in 1864, they were already outnumbered by more than two to one."[289] This was a problem because the newcomers had experienced much less freedom and had exercised little responsibility in their own lives:

> *Many slaves, given a choice, would risk their lives to be free rather than stay on the plantations. More uncertain was their understanding of freedom. Having had far less opportunity to exercise certain degrees of freedom than native blacks of Hampton, would they use it wisely or abuse it and prove the long-standing claim of white Southerners that the black man without slavery was a savage?*[290]

How was the new postwar black community to survive with the original contrabands and the less experienced newcomers sharing space? In addition to eliminating crime from their neighborhoods, black residents had to find constructive occupations for the citizens of their communities. Idleness and the neighborhood saloon proved to be a temptation for some of the freedmen. "A missionary teacher appealed that a 'good temperance man' be sent to

Hampton because it was 'becoming a very wicked place.'"[291] The black community could organize itself and avoid some of those problems. There were already successful black families living in the area. Could a successful black man help another black man from "reverting to savagery" and thus condemning all other black men with him? The answer was found when more black men became literate, acquired higher educations and developed salable skills. The training and discipline required to achieve these goals, along with active participation in the black church, prepared new leaders in the black community. The freedmen of both groups who availed themselves of these opportunities became the black elite of Hampton. They were able to set a standard for the community and see to its enforcement:

> *The black professional group, although small in number, was of vital importance to the black community of Hampton. Members of this group were the acknowledged leaders of the community. They played a large role in shaping the goals and directions of its inhabitants. Anyone who sought respectability within the community had to belong to a church, and it was the ministers who spelled out the norms of acceptable social and religious behavior. Teachers, accepting the Hampton Institute belief in "formative work" among their pupils, did far more than teach reading, writing, and arithmetic. They helped reinforce the norms taught on Sunday in church, and passed on to their students the belief in the importance of education that had typified blacks of Hampton since 1861. Black lawyers played a crucial role in helping blacks acquire property and in protecting them from being cheated out of it once they had it. Black professionals also played another vital, if less concrete, role in shaping the community. They symbolized to the young of the town the heights to which black people might aspire.*[292]

Earlier, however, the harsh conditions in the refugee camps during the Civil War and the absence of meaningful work for both men and women created a situation where the safest reaction was the passive resistance that had been useful on the plantations. Freedom meant having choices, and the ex-slaves during the war had few, if any, real options—there was little chance to practice being free. Those who were given the chance often succeeded:

> *Those freedmen who had the opportunity to rent farms from the Bureau of Negro Affairs, which became possible in the last year and a half of the war, fared better than the others and did much to prove that blacks could support themselves if given the chance...In Elizabeth City County in 1865, 37*

> *farms were rented to 138 tenants and their families. All the farms were reported in good condition and none of the tenants defaulted on their rent payments. Unfortunately, most of the freedmen on the Peninsula never had the opportunity to rent and farm land independently during the war. Those who did were primarily the original contraband from Hampton village.*[293]

When the war ended, black residents had to put their lives together, starting with the basic family unit. Many from the upcountry plantations had been separated from their families and did not know exactly who belonged to whom:

> *The unorthodox familial patterns which the later refugees brought from slavery created more problems for blacks, and for missionaries, than simply determining which wife belonged to which husband. Freedwomen willingly accepted the responsibilities for caring for their children and for keeping proper homes, but not all knew how to do so. On many plantations, one "black mammy" was charged with the care of all slave children. The missionaries continually called for a school to teach the women the habits of "good housewivery* [sic]," *to teach the care and* discipline *of their children. Black freedwomen lacked many of the skills considered to be essential by the missionary ladies. They did not know how to sew, or to cook, or to keep a clean house. More importantly, they lacked knowledge of infant and child care.*[294]

The newly freed black men also faced very real problems. There were fewer jobs to be had, and more men were looking for work. "By 1865, 40,000 freedmen were concentrated on the Peninsula; 7,000 were in the village of Hampton alone...The unclear division of authority between military and civilian agencies fostered the breakdown of civil order. Lawlessness was rampant and clashes between the races were almost daily occurrences."[295] Much of this lawlessness was probably caused by the criminal element from both races. Freedom cannot be enjoyed nor life lived to the fullest in such circumstances. Reasonable people needed to take charge:

> *The priority, second only to defense of freedom itself, became greater social responsibility and stability within their communities. Most freedmen appear to have been supporters, if not active participants, in the armed defense of black settlements and black rights. At the same time, they seemed equally near unanimity in opposing the criminal element among them, black or*

> *white. Much of the theft and violence within postwar black communities was perpetrated by blacks. Black church and political leaders joined forces with the Freedmen's Bureau and even the civil authorities to bring peace to their settlements.*[296]

These settlements were primarily in three areas of Hampton and Elizabeth City County. Property in some parts of town could be bought fairly cheaply and thus was available to the black population. The first was the area known as "Newtown" and was that part of the county bordered on the north by Electric Avenue and on the west by LaSalle Avenue and that extended on the east nearly over to Sunset Creek. "In 1869, Daniel Cock divided a thirty-five acre triangular section of his property into thirty-three lots with the intention of selling the parcels to black buyers. His plat, a drawing by a surveyor which shows individual parcels of land, was titled 'Cock's Newtown.' The first six lots were sold in March of that year for fifty dollars each."[297]

The Little England Chapel was built on a small lot at the edge of Newtown as the neighborhood gathering place. It got its start around 1877 when a teacher from the Normal School noticed three children playing on the beach next to his cottage one Sunday morning. He invited them in, they sang hymns and a Sunday school tradition was begun. By the spring of 1878, 75 people were attending, and "by January 1879, the Sunday School had an enrollment of [110], ranging in age from four to seventy-five."[298] A larger space was definitely needed. A neighborhood fund drive was conducted, and the Normal School president General Armstrong "promised to give one dollar for every four dollars that the neighborhood gave…Daniel Cock offered the use of a small site close to the black community to be used for building a church or a schoolhouse."[299] Thus Newtown gained its own chapel.

Students at the Normal School were encouraged "to provide Christian service to the black neighborhoods near the school…An example was…students [going] across the river to the Newtown neighborhood to teach Sunday School."[300] A more practical assistance was provided when sewing classes were offered in 1889–90:

> *The Normal School ladies cut all the material before taking it to the Little England and Slabtown* [Buckroe] *sewing schools and often pre-basted it as well. The women participating in the classes were required to pay half the price of the material they used. As an incentive, the merchants of the town of Hampton lowered the prices of their goods. The other part of the costs was donated by Northerners interested in supporting a worthy project.*

A class in dressmaking, Hampton Institute, circa 1899. The girls are receiving lessons in sewing and tailoring. They will use these skills to teach the women at Little England Chapel. They also make the male students' uniforms. The men are organized into a corps of cadets and wear a military-style uniform, thus eliminating the need for "proper" college clothes, which few had. *From Engs,* Educating the Disfranchised and Disadvantaged, *photograph courtesy of Library of Congress, LC-USZ62-38151.*

> *The two sewing schools together used fifteen hundred yards of material in a single year, making two hundred sixty garments as well as numerous sheets, towels and other articles. So many women wanted to attend the sewing schools that the buildings could not accommodate all of them.*[301]

A second area of black property ownership was roughly north of Queen Street and west of King Street. The third black settlement was between Fort Monroe and the Soldiers' Home. Both of these properties were put on the market by the court to settle two bankruptcy cases in 1868. At that time,

> *the court-appointed administrators of the estates struck upon the idea of laying out streets and dividing the estates into city lots. The lots were extremely narrow, sometimes only thirty to fifty feet along the street front, and very deep, usually half a block. One group would be most interested in such property, the blacks, and the administrators clearly had them in mind. Prices were very low, sometimes as little as eighty-five dollars; the*

administrators themselves carried the mortgages for many who could not pay the full amount upon purchase.[302]

As these areas were settled, black residents had effectively established their own business and residential communities: "From the beginning of Queen Street at Hampton bridge westward to the end of the then settled area just west of Armistead Avenue, as many as half of all businesses were owned by blacks. A similar pattern existed along King Street northward to the edge of town."[303] The largest store in downtown was a combination grocery and dry goods store owned by Thomas Harmon, a black merchant. Early on, the area was "a ramshackle business district of black-owned boarding-houses, barbershops, eating places, and saloons intermixed with a few imposing structures and homes such as St. John's Church, the Courthouse, and the residences of black sheriff Andrew Williams and black Commissioner of Revenue R.M. Smith."[304] More substantial brick buildings would come later, as the financial affairs of both black and white townspeople improved with the development of the seafood industries and the return of wealthy tourists

"The Fair," an abandoned saloon at the corner of King and Queen Streets, about 1895. This corner at the center of town will soon exhibit a more distinguished aspect. The saloon will be replaced with the more appropriate brick edifice of the Bank of Hampton. *Courtesy of Hampton History Museum, 0372.01.*

to the area. One thing that remained from that early time was the naming of the streets: Grant, Union, Lincoln and Liberty indicate choices of the black population. The school that the area children attended was the Lincoln School. The court plan of selling the second estate in small lots worked as well in the new settlement across Mill Creek from Fort Monroe, which came to be called Phoebus.

Black residents were now property owners, and jobs were available in construction, skilled crafts—such as blacksmiths and shoemakers—and the seafood industry.[305] With the establishment of the black church, the community had taken responsibility for its own self-improvement: "One of their first cooperative acts was to institutionalize [religion] in separate churches under their own control. In 1863 they founded Zion Baptist Church at Hampton…and First Baptist Church of Hampton."[306] These were not the missionary-led organizations of ex-slaves. The freedmen had discovered real choices: "Freedom meant the right to control one's own life, to pray in one's own way, and to suffer the consequences of one's own mistakes….black acceptance of [the missionary] values came only after most missionaries had departed and blacks could make the choice because of their own needs, rather than because of needs imposed upon them."[307]

THE HAMPTON NORMAL AND AGRICULTURAL INSTITUTE

Like the Soldiers' Home, the Hampton Normal and Agricultural Institute would never have come into existence except as a result of the Civil War. The people who would be the founders of the school and those who would attend the classes came together during the conflict and stayed during the period of transition that followed. The American Missionary Association came to Hampton in 1861 to assist the newly freed slaves and remained throughout the war as teachers to the black population. When the war ended, the AMA continued its emphasis on education as a way to "uplift" the freedmen. To train black teachers, the AMA "in 1867 and 1868, founded eight teacher-training schools in Macon, Savannah and Atlanta, Georgia; Charleston, South Carolina; Louisville, Kentucky; Nashville, Tennessee; Talladega, Alabama; and Hampton, Virginia."[308]

From the beginning, the school in Hampton was different from the others, due to the character of its first principal and the goals he established for the institute.[309] Samuel Chapman Armstrong had served in the Union army and came to Hampton after the war as the local director of the Freedmen's Bureau. The bureau's main task was to aid the ex-slaves in their transition to freedom, and an essential part of that task was to develop local educational facilities. Armstrong was literally placed in the midst of the two things that would occupy him for the rest of his life: black youth and their education. His vision of a school to train the newly freed black youth was based on his army experience and missionary training:

> *First, his military experience, and his success in it, had persuaded him that blacks needed a more rigid, disciplined educational environment than other missionaries advocated. Second, his upbringing as his father's assistant in organizing schools for indigenous Hawaiians had wedded him to the idea of "industrial education" as a primary means of advancement for "backward peoples." Third, that same background had inspired in him a grandiose notion of "saving races." Thus he set out to design a system that would give the black masses at least a rudimentary education.*[310]

Before he could lead such a school, however, he had to be asked; the AMA was in charge. First, he pushed for the purchase of land in Hampton and finessed the AMA into buying the property: "The site agreed upon was 125 acres of a former plantation called Little Scotland, or, less elegantly, Wood's Farm."[311] Despite being on hand and available, Armstrong had to wait until the first person offered the position of principal declined, whereupon he readily accepted the offer. The Hampton Normal and Agricultural Institute opened on April 6, 1868, with Samuel Chapman Armstrong in charge.[312]

The April opening of the school was an auspicious occasion, but "in 1868, the new Hampton Institute was not much to look at. It consisted of some old army barracks, the remnants of Chesapeake Army Hospital, and the decrepit mansion house of the former Little Scotland plantation."[313] All that would change as Armstrong set about acquiring financial support:

> *In March, 1872, the General Assembly of Virginia passed an Act, giving the institution one-third of the Agricultural College land grant of Virginia. Its share was one hundred thousand acres, which were sold in May, 1872, for $95,000. Nine-tenths of this money was invested in State bonds, bearing six per cent interest; the other tenth has been expended in the purchase of additional land, increasing the size of the home farm to one hundred and ninety acres.*[314]

Hampton Institute campus, 1899. On a calm winter day, the buildings of the Normal School stand out against the sky. *From left to right*: Principal's House, Memorial Chapel and Clock Tower, Academic Hall and the Huntington Industrial Works. The pier and boathouse are in the center. *Courtesy of Library of Congress LC-USZ62-68930.*

After acquiring the land grant and the much-needed funds, 'the Institute was virtually independent of the American Missionary Association."[315] By 1885, the "entire property of the School is…valued at about $400,000, most of which has been paid for by private contributions."[316] The large brick buildings of the 1880s campus were constructed in part from money received as gifts from those Northern benefactors.

The essential purpose of the Hampton Normal School was to train black teachers who would then go out into the hinterland of the South and teach black students. The curriculum of a "Normal" school was built around this idea: "During their three years—the "Junior," "Middle," and "Senior"—students completed the equivalent of a high school education… Seniors were required to engage in practice teaching at the 'Butler School' for black youngsters on Hampton's campus."[317] There was one very important addition to the course of study in Hampton; it also incorporated a trade school requirement:

> *Southern black schools usually were in session less than six months a year. Hampton alumni needed to learn other skills simply to support themselves and their families during the remaining months. In short, manual labor education at Hampton was, originally, a means to important ends. It would provide graduates with moral character and additional skills needed so that they could pursue their primary task of teaching others.*[318]

Hampton was also unusual in that it was coeducational and emphasized a "home" atmosphere where moral values would be learned within the institute family:

> *Armstrong believed that immorality was a major weakness of the black race. Therefore, women would have to play an equal role in uplifting the black race. By teaching men and women together under the close supervision of their teachers, the school could inculcate the habits and values that had to be passed on to their pupils and communities.*[319]

The black students seem to have taken all this in stride; they were young, away from home for the first time and making new friends. They were probably enjoying themselves as college students always have. As they became more sophisticated, many realized that they could acquire an education and later decide on their own goals in life. "It is true that most of them became teachers, but very few were *only* teachers. They were also lawyers; they were

Class in capillary physics at Hampton Institute. Female students have joined the men in what appears to be a physics lab. The men are wearing the uniform of the cadet corps. *http://hdl.loc.gov/loc.pnp/cph.3c08065, courtesy of Library of Congress, LC-USZ62-108065.*

ministers, newspaper editors, actors, musicians, Pullman porters, postal workers, and politicians...about 10 percent went on to advanced training in northern white schools."[320]

Three different aspects of the early Hampton Normal School experience are given special attention here: the Trade School Course, the Indian School and Regulations for both male and female students. The Trade School was greatly needed to give the students a source of income: "Most of Hampton's early students were like the young Booker T. Washington, who simply arrived at Hampton's gates and sought acceptance."[321] They could not pay for their education nor support themselves while in attendance: "Students' labor is generally faithful, but school boys' work is not equal to that of hired hands. It is, however, paid at the price of the latter, regardless of the demand for it, not only as needed stimulus but as necessary to their support."[322] Courses were added to the curriculum to provide that work. The Trade School Course was developed in 1879:

> *It was four years in length. During the first three of those years, boys spent forty-nine hours a week in "Shop Practice" and a total of sixteen hours in academic pursuits, along with eight hours in activities such as mechanical drawing, mechanics, gymnastics/drill, and trade discussion. Additionally, they spent twelve hours a week in "Supervised Study." Only in the fourth year did students spend the bulk of their time pursuing the Normal Course curriculum.*[323]

By 1884, the school owned two large farms, a sawmill, a machine shop, a carpenter shop, a harness shop, a tin shop, a paint shop and a shoe shop, and a wheelwright and blacksmith were operating on campus. The uses for these are self-explanatory and would offer students a wide choice of trades. All of the equipment, buildings and instruction were expensive and also needed the infusion of Northern money. The girls were offered training suitable to their sex that would be useful in their future lives as teachers and housewives. In the Stone Memorial Building, "we come first to the Girls' Industrial Room and Sewing and Tailoring Department. Here all the mending and making of garments is done, and uniforms for the students are made...On the same floor we come to the Knitting Department. Here the manufacture of mittens is carried on. The products of this department are taken by a firm in Massachusetts."[324] The girls who led the sewing classes at Little England Chapel would have received their own training here.

One of the trades is of special interest: the Printing Office and Book Bindery. This department was run as an actual business and printed several magazines as well as the Soldiers' Home weekly newspaper, the *Soldiers' Home Bulletin*. A business such as this had to meet deadlines and work on a schedule. An official staff was employed to do most of the work, with from twelve to fifteen boys as assistants. The office was a good example of using your best resources, wherever they can be found; several veterans from the Soldiers' Home were at work, "while the book-binder also wears the uniform of Uncle Sam."[325]

The logical outlet for the items produced in the various trades and crafts was the village of Hampton, and that meant competition for the local businesses. The institute's local alumni came to the aid of their school when charges were brought to that effect: "It was the black delegates in the legislature and black merchants in Hampton village who led the defense in refuting charges in 1886 and 1887 that the Institute's various shops constituted an illegal restraint on local trade."[326] Things probably evened out over the long run, as the students were allowed to shop in town once a week.

That the Trade School was successful in the early years at Hampton can be seen in the career of one of its best-known graduates. Booker T. Washington, class of 1875, "began his education in a prototype of what evolved into the [Trade] School, and he later came back to oversee it."[327] His work as president of Tuskegee Institute showed that he had absorbed both the lessons and goals of Hampton Institute and that he endeavored to replicate them in rural Alabama.

Since the students could not pay for their tuition, room and board, Principal Armstrong had to acquire funding elsewhere. As has been noted, money came to the institute from Northern benefactors. It is interesting to see how those connections were made. Armstrong had a "product" to sell: his school for black ex-slaves. To draw attention to the uniqueness of his program, he "borrowed an idea from Hampton's sister AMA school, Fisk University in Nashville. Armstrong created a choral group, 'The Hampton Singers,' modeled after Fisk's successful 'Jubilee Choir.'"[328] As in many other things relating to the school, Armstrong devoted his full attention to the development of his choir: "Armstrong traveled about Virginia with his music director, Thomas Fenner, searching for talented singers in the fields and in the tobacco factories of Richmond."[329] Once the choir was assembled and trained, the group went on tour to the major Northeastern cities to raise money:

> *The tour was a grand success. The group received rave reviews in Troy, Rochester, and New York City. It did not fare quite as well in Boston, apparently because the concert followed a disastrous 1872 fire in that*

> *city, and philanthropists were giving their money to a cause closer to home. The tour continued on through Philadelphia and reached its climax as the "Singers" performed in the Capitol Rotunda and before President Ulysses S. Grant on the White House steps.*[330]

Virginia Hall, the largest building on campus, was completed in 1874, "partly through the efforts of the 'Hampton Singers,' in a three year's [*sic*] singing campaign."[331] Armstrong's choir had achieved success and fulfilled its purpose: the moneyed elite of the Northeast now knew and approved of this Southern black school.

In April 1878, the first Native Americans arrived at Hampton from the western plains by way of Florida:

> *In 1874, some 150 Kiowa, Comanche, and Arapaho Indians who had participated in an uprising in the Indian Territory of Oklahoma were incarcerated at Fort Marion, Florida. Their warden was Lt. Richard Henry Pratt, a United States Army officer who had commanded black troops during the Civil War. The exiled Indians had been imprisoned without regard to actual guilt in the uprising. Such injustice outraged Pratt. He barraged officials in Washington with letters begging for the release of those who were innocent and for some provision for "civilizing" the others. Finally, in 1877, the army and then Indian Commissioner E.A. Hayt agreed to the release of Pratt's charges and to their education in eastern schools if they desired it.*[332]

Samuel Armstrong decided to add another of the "backward races" to his educational program, and Lieutenant Pratt accepted the offer, since "eastern whites wanted no part of Pratt's partially tamed 'savages.'"[333] Hampton Normal School gained not only a new teaching challenge but also a financial boost. "The United States pays $167 a piece per annum toward the board and clothes of 120 Indians; allowing nothing for tuition, [which costs about $70 each per annum], or for buildings for their accommodation, for which, about $50,000 have been paid by the school. For this sum, amounting to about $35,000 annually, the School looks to the friends of both races."[334] A new worthy project was offered to those wealthy friends, and they must have come through. The school would eventually build two separate dormitories for the Native American students, the Wigwam for the men and Winona Lodge for the women. Coeducation was deemed essential for the "uplift" of the Indian, as it was for the black students.

Armstrong and his staff tried to blend the two groups of students into one community, but the differences were too great. For one thing, most of the Native Americans knew very little English and had only a rudimentary education when they came to the school. A separate program had to be established. "The first three years of the Indian School program concerned 'oral training in English,' with rudiments of writing. Only in the fourth year did students actually begin to study texts. History, mathematics, geography, and art also were included in the curriculum. The Indian students…had particular difficulty with mathematical concepts."[335]

Another problem appeared early in the experiment: the men of the two races did not like one another. The black men were not sure that the Native American men were sufficiently "tamed," and the Native Americans felt superior to the black men.[336] These were differences that could not be solved in an academic setting, and eventually, two separate schools were formed. As part of their training, Native American students were also required to learn manual skills, and in 1887, they "studied in a 'technical shop', in which they received a modest amount of training in a variety of trades."[337] The Native American women worked with the black women in housekeeping skills:

> *The Indian men were organized in separate companies of the school cadet corps and were inspected daily by student officers. As with black students, the process of teaching civilization continued into the evenings. Indian students attended their required study halls and participated in their own debate society, prayer meetings, temperance association, and social events at Winona Lodge. On special occasions, such as Founders' Day, they joined the black students in social affairs.*[338]

A problem occurred in the lives of the Native American students that was unrelated to attitude or aptitude; many became sick in the hot, humid climate of southeastern Virginia. They had grown up in the high western plains and "were described as suffering from 'weak lungs.' They frequently were plagued by scrofula, an early manifestation of tuberculosis, and many of them later contracted pneumonia and tuberculosis."[339] The school staff tried its best to help the students entrusted to its care by creating a separate kitchen and dining room to cater to their special needs: "Even these precautions were not entirely sufficient; of the 427 Indian students who attended Hampton between 1878 and 1888, 31 died. Another 111 had to be returned to their reservations because of poor health."[340]

The Indian School at Hampton Institute was designed as a five-year program. Unfortunately, the government scholarships were for three years of study, so most American Indian students returned to their reservations with only a smattering of proper education. There was not enough work for the men back home, and "the vast majority of Hampton's Indian male graduates became subsistence farmers. An overwhelming majority of the women became the wives of such men and the mothers of their children."[341] A few students went on to graduate programs in medicine, teaching or law and returned to work with their own people.

In 1912, the government subsidy was removed and "so brought about the demise of Hampton's Indian School. Indians, though in much smaller numbers, continued to attend the institute for another decade, supported by private charities."[342] The attempt to form the two races into one community could not be termed a success, but it is to be hoped that they gained something positive from the experience.

General Armstrong's idea of a rigid, disciplined educational experience for the students at the Normal School was worked out in detail. The goal was not only to educate but also to prepare the young black students to succeed in the white society around them. They would need self-discipline to survive:

> *Accordingly, Hampton's teachers instituted a rigid set of behavioral regulations and an almost draconian disciplinary system. Hampton students were regimented from "Rising Bell" at 5:15 A.M. until "Taps" or "Lights-out" at 9:30. Each half hour or hour of their day was programmed. After breakfast at 6 A.M., their rooms were inspected. They attended chapel twice daily. Male students were organized into a corps of cadets. Uniforms were required of all male students* [a boon for many of them who otherwise could not have afforded decent clothing]. *The men marched to classes, meals, and work details. Women were not so regimented, but were supervised as closely by their teachers and matrons in the dormitories. Students were allowed only one afternoon a week to go into nearby Hampton village for necessities, a day carefully chosen so that it did not coincide with "market day," when local rowdies might be around to corrupt them.*[343]

The students who could not accommodate themselves to such a program were disciplined by receiving demerits. "Excessive demerits could result in fines [an impractical device, since most students had no money]; exile to the almost primitive conditions on the school farm at Shellbanks, several miles from the campus; or incarceration in the campus guardhouse."[344] The idea of a school "jail" sounds extreme today, but it must have been better than calling in the civil authorities from the town of Hampton. The main idea was to save as many young black people as possible, and the institute succeeded in that.

The village of Hampton in particular benefitted from its graduates, who came home to teach in the new black public schools. They also pursued professions in the "ministry and the law, both of which usually led to political involvement as well."[345] Black men were elected to office in the town and county, and to the Virginia legislature. Some became merchants, and John Mallory Phillips founded his own seafood industry. Its graduates signaled the success of the Hampton Normal and Agricultural Institute.

12

Changing Lifestyles

The Civil War changed many things; peoples' lives were vastly different from what they had been just a generation before. The Hickman children who had lived on the farm called Pleasantville didn't dwell on the past or on things that were now gone completely. They got on with their lives, took advantage of opportunities as they cropped up and became involved in the new town that was rising around them. There was no lamenting over what might have been or the "Lost Cause" of the Confederacy. Once or twice I heard Granny sing "The Bonnie Blue Flag," but it was a cheerful rendition. I don't know the proper tune, but Granny sang it as it is notated on page 142.[346]

The blue flag with the one white star was one of several Confederate flags: "The single star represented secession, the removal of a star from the Stars and Stripes, and independence in that it stood alone on a field of blue."[347] The song was popular during the war, and there are many verses, but all that Granny sang was the refrain. The old veterans at the Soldiers' Home would put on their uniforms occasionally and march in a parade, but there was not a burning desire to return to whatever the glory days were that some imagined had existed. Those men knew too well what war was like.

Family relationships and traditions were the important things carried over to this new generation. In the Hickman family, sisters and brothers lived near one another. At weddings, a brother was best man, and cousins were bridesmaids; at funerals, everyone was there. If anyone was to live alone or needed help, someone came to stay. When a young parent died or was very ill, a sister took in the children, and when necessary, an uncle became a legal

Music notation for "The Bonnie Blue Flag." *Notation by Randy Cabell.*

guardian. Churchgoing was more than just a formality. The family members were not "paragons of virtue," and one or two in my generation didn't turn out too well, but for the most part, the children of the farm did the things that needed to be done and did them for the right reasons

Granny used to say that one generation plants for the next. The truth of that statement is evidenced by the pecan tree on Cherokee Road and the live oaks on the farm. I also have bulbs in my yard that originally came from Granny's house. The jonquils and narcissus were planted in long rows in her backyard, and the spider lilies and blue scillas lined the brick walk that led to her front door. After researching this story, I can say that the planting of values and relationships was also a priority for the family and that they succeeded in this as well.

Women's changing lifestyles were a prominent aspect of this new generation. Black women were able to work for wages outside their homes, and many did so. Opportunities were available in the seafood industry, the resort hotels and as servants. Hampton Institute women taught school and took leadership positions in their communities and churches. The lives of white women at this time were more circumscribed. Teaching was acceptable, as had been demonstrated early on when the women of the American Missionary Association came from the Northeast to teach in the freedmen's schools. Teaching in the public schools of Virginia, however, was limited to single women. A few women worked in a family business or as telephone operators later on when the phone system was installed. Other than that, church work was about the limit of activity outside "keeping house" and child rearing.

Illnesses and infant mortality were still very much a part of everyday experience. The five Hickman girls who married lost a total of ten children as newborns or as very young children. Two of those mothers also died as a result of childbirth complications. Diphtheria and consumption, or tuberculosis, were often the causes of deaths in children. Granny's daughter Mary, who was called May, died at age two of diphtheria.

Virginia did begin a statewide health system on a small scale in 1860 with the enactment of a law to permit the vaccination of the poor by the county overseers responsible for their care. The Civil War intervened, and it wasn't until 1872 that the State Board of Health in Virginia was created. In 1882, municipal authorities were authorized to require vaccinations as, for example, a requirement to attend the public schools. In 1895, a law was passed whereby prisoners with contagious diseases would be quarantined. It wasn't until 1896 that, for the first time, the State of Virginia appropriated money to fund the State Board of Health; the amount was $2,000.[348]

There were at least two instances of quarantine and epidemic illness in Hampton in the late 1800s: "One of the few times they [Hampton Normal School students] were known to miss Sunday services was when all the missionary schools were temporarily closed at the end of 1887 because of an outbreak of measles."[349] A more serious situation put the town of Hampton under quarantine in 1899: "Disease hampered student missionary work during the spring of 1899 when smallpox broke out in the locality at the end of winter, lasting until mid-spring. The young missionaries were kept in isolation on the campus and so were unable to visit individuals or conduct their usual Sunday School classes."[350] There are stories told about young people in the town trying to escape the quarantine by rowing out into Hampton Roads and flagging a passing boat to take them up the James to visit relatives. At least one of those stories is likely true.

Health services were available in Hampton, but there was no central healthcare system for all citizens. In answer to that need, the Dixie Hospital received its charter in 1892 from the Virginia General Assembly. The hospital's founder was Alice Bacon, "the daughter of the distinguished Congregational minister, Leonard Bacon, of New Haven's First Church."[351] While a member of the Normal School's faculty, she would visit the sick in the neighborhood and was concerned about the unsanitary conditions often found there. By 1890, Miss Bacon had resolved to establish a hospital in which "we can nurse the sick who cannot be cared for in their own homes."[352] Hampton Institute approved the plan and "donated an old carpentry shop on the grounds of the school"[353] for that purpose. Miss Bacon was then able to start a nursing program for the female students, since there would now be a hospital in which they could practice their skills:

The Hampton Training School for nurses provided health care to the local sick, as well as an opportunity for professional training for black women. Few such opportunities existed for either black or white women of the time.

> *Nursing, though strenuous, was attractive to young women because it offered security and prestige because of its high moral purpose. It also provided women the rare chance to attain executive status, as a hospital superintendent or director of nursing. At the time that Miss Bacon established her school and hospital, there were hundreds of training schools across the country. Of these, only one other nursing school in the country accepted blacks.*[354]

The origin of the name "Dixie" for the new hospital is something of a mystery. Miss Bacon's horse by that name would be hitched to the wagon that served as the ambulance, and that sight became familiar in the town. "Dixie" became associated with the hospital, and the nickname seems to have stuck. Regardless of the name, the hospital was a success. In the first year, "thirty-seven patients were treated in the two-room building, with a resident physician, a superintendent of nurses, and five students." Illnesses and other health concerns could now be addressed more directly, and the Town of Hampton was the beneficiary.

As people's lifestyles changed, there was more time for relaxation. The area's beaches were attractive and situated on the beautiful Chesapeake

Buckroe beach with bathers and fishing pier, 1905. Local families as well as visitors from Richmond enjoyed the beach at Buckroe. The shallower water seems to be marked here by the striped pole. Nonbathers could watch from the covered pavilion or stroll along the pier where there are benches scattered along its length. *Courtesy of Hampton History Museum, 2009.15.6231.*

Bay, so entrepreneurs soon began to capitalize on that fact. Day trips were popular and possible because of the streetcar line that had been extended to Buckroe. "In 1883, Mary Ann Dobbins Herbert acquired part of the Buckroe Plantation and opened a boardinghouse for summer guests."[355] A bathhouse and a dance pavilion were added, and the beach became more than a place to swim in good weather. J.S. Darling bought land and added a hotel to his business enterprises. The Buckroe Beach Hotel opened in time for the summer trade in 1897. By the early twentieth century, Buckroe had "become a popular middle-class retreat for Richmond residents."[356] With the addition of extra-heavy rails to the trolley tracks, visitors from Richmond could ride the excursion trains right up to the beachfront.

This was a time of racial segregation, and a hotel, the Bayshore, was built in 1898 for black visitors to the area. The hotel overlooked the bay and the stretch of beach between Fort Monroe and Buckroe. It was an extremely successful business undertaking and was popular well into the mid-1900s. Another beach hotel for the white population was built in 1890, just a few miles up the beach from Buckroe at Grand View, near Fox Hill.[357] You used to be able to walk along the water between those two places and wade or swim across the inlet to the Salt Ponds. The difference between wading or swimming depended on the tide.

13

1907

A Red-Letter Year for Hampton

By 1907, when the whole area was preparing for the 300th celebration of the founding of Jamestown, Hampton was again a thriving town, with substantial brick buildings and homes sharing space in downtown. People came to shop and conduct business. On Saturday and Sunday, religious services were held in the synagogue and in the many churches. The town was successfully reconstructed.

In August 1907, in commemoration of the exposition, the local newspaper published an *Industrial Number of the* Hampton Monitor. The book contains a great many advertisements displaying the goods and services offered by the citizens and merchants of Hampton. It also includes a long essay that lists the assets and advantages of his hometown as seen by the editor. Of the physical characteristics described, the editor begins in 1891 when the "first trolley car from Newport News to Old Point Comfort passed through the city. The streets were illuminated by electricity."[358] Court Street was paved in 1900. The YMCA was organized in 1888 and grew rapidly; Dr. Thomas H. Parramore was the first president of the board of directors. The *Hampton Monitor* was established in 1886 and, in 1905, moved to the Kecoughtan Building on South King Street.[359]

Of particular interest to the citizens of Hampton was the new water system. The Newport News Light and Water Company was organized in 1892, and in 1895, the water mains were extended to Hampton and Old Point. The reservoir was in Lee Hall, where there was a new filtering system and pumping station: "The Peninsula from Newport News to Old Point is

The corner of King and Queen Streets, looking south, circa 1905. The residents of Hampton have come a long way in rebuilding their town. This was the area burned to the ground in 1861. At the far end of the street is the busy King Street wharf, and substantial brick buildings and shade trees line the road. A carriage is parked by the bank, and the horse is patiently waiting for its owner to complete the business of the day. *Courtesy of Hampton History Museum, 2009.15.6489.*

peculiarly fortunate in having a corporation in its midst that stands ready to supply at the minimum cost, clear health giving water."[360]

Local farms and their ability to supply produce to the large cities of the East were given prominent space in the essay. After the one-crop tobacco economy had ruined the soil, Virginia farmers had improved their land and now produced a variety of crops. "This section now furnishes a tremendous amount of truck [farming] in the way of Irish potatoes, beans, peas, cabbage, lettuce, carrots, corn, onions and tomatoes."[361] These were harvested and then "shipped across the Roads to Norfolk. From there they were exported daily to New York aboard Old Dominion Line steamships which made the run to New York in twenty-four hours. In the spring of each year, ships sailed daily loaded with nothing but fresh strawberries bound for the New York and Philadelphia markers."[362]

Seafood received its share of attention as the area's largest industry and leading source of tax revenue: "The total tax received from the oyster planters,

Chesapeake Bay log canoe about 1900. This boat coming out of Hampton River is making the best of a light breeze by sailing "wing and wing." The sailor is Matt Armstrong, who lived across from the Normal School. Matt's brother Samuel was the first principal of the school. *Courtesy of Hampton History Museum, 1968.2.1.*

crab, clam and other fish dealers for the present year was $6,084.15."[363] The oyster companies, led by J.S. Darling and Son, headed the list, and "the three leading dealers of Hampton ship about 300,000 gallons [of oysters] annually."[364] The crabbing business owned by McMenamin & Company employed over 350 men and women at the plant, and fifty or sixty boats worked the crab lines in the busy season: "It is a sight worth seeing to watch the boats of this fleet in the early dawn of a summer morning set sail for the fishing grounds, returning in the evening in tow of a tug, 15 or 20 in line laden to the bows with the delicious crustaceans."[365]

The newspaper editor ended the essay by identifying the Bank of Hampton as a very valuable asset: "The oldest as well as the largest banking institution in Hampton or the Peninsula is the Bank of Hampton, one of the best known and strongest banks in the State…No other one institution perhaps has had so much to do with the growth of Hampton as this bank and it is now, as it has been for years, one of the staunchest bulwarks of the city's prosperity."[366] The bank's list of directors for 1907 reads like a "Who's Who" of the entire town: Henry Lane Schmelz, George A. Schmelz, F.W.

Darling, Jacob Heffelfinger, A. Howe, W.W. Richardson, J.T. Lee, J.B. Lake, J.C. Robinson, John B. Kimberly, S. Gordon Cumming, Nelson S. Groome."[367] The *Hampton Monitor* editor was proud of his town and published its attractions to compete with all the publicity surrounding the official Jamestown Exposition in Norfolk.

The Town of Hampton had the same thing in mind when the Jamestown advertising committee was called to order by chairman Henry L. Schmelz on January 14, 1907: "At this meeting the preliminary steps looking to raising $4,000 for advertising Hampton, Phoebus and Elizabeth City County during the exposition will be taken up and a course of soliciting the funds mapped out."[368]

Hampton already had a first-class resort hotel ready to receive visitors to the 300th grand celebration. The new Chamberlin Hotel had replaced the Hygeia as the epitome of style and gracious living. It was built on Old Point Comfort adjacent to Fort Monroe, and for a while, the two hostelries occupied the waterfront side by side. The older Hygeia suffered in comparison and went into a decline, finally being demolished in the spring of 1904. The Chamberlin, meanwhile, was at the peak of its popularity. It had opened in April 1896 and was advertised as being "among the largest and the most attractive of America's hostelries."[369] The Chamberlin was now the center of social activity on Old Point and was well situated to host visitors to the exposition. Those visitors could enjoy the pleasant breezes off the water and have a front row seat for viewing the parade of ships coming into the harbor. The deep-water channel ran between Old Point and the Rip Raps, so all the international fleet would pass by in review right off shore. For those who wished to travel across the harbor to attend the festivities, "two ferries ran from Old Point Comfort through the assembled fleet and then on to Sewell's Point, where sightseers enjoyed the exhibits."[370]

The Hampton publicity campaign must have worked well. The lead local story in the *Daily Press* on March 9 was that the congressional delegation from Washington would stay on the Hampton side of the harbor: "The United States Senators and Congressmen, who will represent the government at the opening of the Jamestown Exposition, will have their headquarters at Hotel Chamberlin during their stay on the Virginia Peninsula."[371] The newspaper also played its role in keeping the exposition news current. On March 21, there was a headline with no story that read "Jamestown Exposition Opens in Thirty-three days."[372]

As the opening day approached, activity increased in the harbor: "The battleship *Louisiana* headed the fleet of 14 big battleships and two immense armored cruisers…They steamed into Hampton Roads about 6:15 o'clock

First Chamberlin Hotel from Old Point Comfort Wharf. The elegant building has waterfront views from three sides and has direct access to the Old Point Wharf. Visitors could arrive by steamboat for their vacations at the seaside. *Courtesy of Hampton History Museum, 2009.15.2409.*

The wharf at Old Point Comfort, 1907. The wharf was a busy place during the opening days of the Jamestown Exposition. Steamboats made their regular trips across Hampton Roads and also took passengers to Sewell's Point and the exposition grounds. The trolley cars have brought visitors to board the steamer and the smaller boats moored alongside the wharf. The president's yacht *Mayflower* is out in the channel. *Courtesy of Hampton History Museum, 1983.26.5.*

The *Mayflower* at Old Point Comfort, 1907. In this view of the wharf at Old Point, many people have arrived and boarded the boats for the Jamestown Exposition. The *Mayflower* is coming into the harbor, and the sailing yacht is decorated for the occasion. *Courtesy of Library of Congress, Prints & Photographs Division, Detroit Publishing Company Collection, LC-D4-22399.*

yesterday afternoon and dropped anchor…between Old Point Comfort and Sewell's Point."[373] People living along the Boulevard in Hampton could row or sail out to watch the fleet come in or, like the Parramore family, take a picnic down the street to the McMenamin pier and watch in comfort. It was indeed a sight to behold, with the entire harbor filled with large warships, including the American ships that were painted white for the event. My mother was ten years old that summer, and she remembered very clearly how impressive the Great White Fleet was.

It was becoming evident that the real message of the Jamestown Exposition put before the public was the military might of the United States. This interpretation was given even more credence when "Fort Monroe Guns to be Well-Guarded" was the headline of the *Daily Press* on April 18. The federal government had employed ten private detectives to assist the army in patrolling Fort Monroe during the exposition. The detectives "will look after foreigners to see that no unauthorized persons get within the new fortifications guarding the entrance to Hampton Roads…Hampton Roads is one of the four most important coast artillery posts in the country."[374]

U.S. fleet in Hampton Roads, 1907. The Virginia-class battleships shown here are part of the Great White Fleet that assembled in Hampton Roads for the exposition. So many ships came from around the world that an anchorage blueprint had to be prepared. *Courtesy of Library of Congress, Prints & Photographs Division, Detroit Publishing Company Collection, LC-D4-22397.*

McMenamin House pier from the water. The pier was used by the whole neighborhood for fishing, crabbing or just watching the fascinating activity unfolding on the water. Several adults and a child are seen in this picture. The black woman wearing an apron and leaning on the railing is probably Lucy Slaughter, who helped raise the three McMenamin children after their parents died. *Courtesy of Hampton History Museum, 2008.33.8.*

The town of Hampton was ready to participate in the festivities. The "Town Council will make [April] 26th a holiday" ran one headline, and another declared that "the town of Phoebus will run a direct ferry line between Phoebus and the Exposition."[375] The big day arrived with the firing of three hundred guns to commemorate the 300th anniversary of the founding of America and then a twenty-one-gun salute to mark the arrival of President Theodore Roosevelt aboard the presidential yacht, the *Mayflower.* The president pressed the golden button later that afternoon, and the Jamestown Tercentennial Exposition was officially open.[376]

U.S. battleships saluting the *Mayflower*, Hampton Roads, 1907. The ships are giving the traditional twenty-one-gun salute. President Theodore Roosevelt is on board the *Mayflower* at the center right of the picture. *Courtesy of Library of Congress, Prints & Photographs Division, Detroit Publishing Company Collection, LC-D4-22398.*

The exposition would not close until November, but long before then, the excitement had worn off. The U.S. warships came and went from Hampton Roads during the summer as, two or three at a time, they put out to sea for gunnery practice. Then, on December 16, 1907, President Roosevelt's Great White Fleet of warships left the harbor for a "show of force" trip around the world.[377] Forty thousand miles of sea travel and two years later, the fleet returned to Hampton Roads for the last time as an armada.[378] For the town of Hampton, the whole exposition affair was a trial run. In three years' time, Hampton would celebrate its own 300th anniversary, and it would be a satisfying, rather than a spectacular, hometown affair.

14

Coming Home

Afterward

Those who had been children on the farm had established their own homes, had children of their own and were part of a new generation. The grandchildren, now the second generation out from the farm, were the last to stay relatively close to home. Two world wars and the evolving of a more mobile society meant that families were now scattered around the world. For this family, however, there does seem to be a connecting thread, which I call a sense of place—a belonging. Our roots were set deeply in the town of Hampton: we knew people, the creeks and the waterfront were part of our earliest experiences, the land had sustained the family for generations. All these things drew us back home.

Perhaps this is a good place to provide some background about my family. My father had been a cavalry officer and later a member of the signal corps stationed at Langley Field on what had been the Booker property called Sherwood. Mother was his secretary, and they were married in October 1918. Jimmy, Mary Louise, Bill and Angeline rounded out the family in 1934, when Daddy was asked to take command of two CCC (Civilian Conservation Corps) camps, the white camp in Petersburg and the black camp in Waverly. The house on Cherokee Road was rented out, and the Matthews family moved to Petersburg. I was born the next year and thrown into the mix. By the summer of 1939, the Depression was easing and the CCC camps were closing. We packed up our belongings and came back to Hampton. Jimmy was almost twenty, Mary Louise was eighteen, Bill was fifteen and Angeline was twelve. I was not quite four, but I was not "the

This is a typical Tidewater marsh and creek. The area is a haven for wildlife, from crabs and fish to deer, small animals and birds of every sort. A creek is more sheltered than open water and thus has always been the choice home site of people since the days of the Kicotan Indians. *Author's collection.*

baby of the family"; I was expected to participate in whatever was going on. A few days after our return, Jimmy asked me to go down to the beach and check on the tide because he wanted to go sailing. Our house was a block down Cherokee from Chesapeake Avenue, so I walked to the Boulevard and looked at the water. I went back home and told Jimmy, "I don't know." He then explained very patiently that a ship has an anchor chain on its bow and thus swings with the tide. If the ship is pointing at Fort Monroe, the tide is coming in; if it is pointing at Newport News, the tide is going out. I took my new knowledge back down to the beach and returned to announce with assurance that the tide was coming in. That experience is now so much a part of who I am that I cannot drive across a creek in Williamsburg or ride a train crossing a river in Connecticut without checking the tide.

Granny's son Thomas, my uncle Tom, had lived in California for twenty or more years. After World War II was over, he came home to visit. One of the first things he wanted to do was to go soft crabbing. He took me with him, and we went out from Uncle Paul's on Indian River Creek. Back then, the creek still had its real mouth, west of the one dredged through the sand spit. We put on old tennis shoes, took a hand net and a basket and started off.

Sailboat with lanteen rig. Granny's son Tom Parramore is seen here sailing out into Hampton Roads. Like most Hamptonians, the family owned a sailboat and kept it close at hand for ready use. This boat was anchored by the McMenamin pier at the end of Cherokee Road. *Courtesy of Hampton History Museum, 2008.33.2.*

It was as if Uncle Tom had never left. He taught me to identify a "buster" and how to keep track of it until it had shed, to look in all the likely places to find the most crabs and, most of all, to enjoy being on the water, following the tide out to the sand bars.

Daisy McMenamin was the second daughter of John and Dorothy McMenamin. She had served in the Women's Army Corps in World War II and later returned to make her home in Hampton. She never married and kept very much up-to-date on what was happening worldwide, as well as things of more local interest. She would write letters to the newspaper expressing an intelligent view of the matter at hand. Sometimes there would be an acerbic bite to the letter when she would take a stand on a controversial local issue. She was entitled to her opinion; she really cared about the old town of Hampton. She had come home. She belonged.

Charles Hickman Wood had been to VPI (Virginia Tech) and had a good job at the shipyard. He was an outdoor sort of man, however, and felt confined in a day-after-day routine. He already owned land near where the poorhouse used to be and made a smooth transition from electrical engineer to peach farmer. His daughter Judy remembers that when she was very young, the family sold peaches under a tent set up at the foot of their lane off Linden Street. Linden is one of those streets whose names were changed after the 1952 merger of the town of Hampton and Elizabeth City County. Today, it is known as Boxwood Street in East Hampton. Sometime around 1943, Charles started a business on what was then a new road called Military Highway. That road was built during the Second World War to connect Fort Monroe and Fort Eustis. It is now called Mercury Boulevard after the original seven astronauts who trained at NASA in the Mercury Program. The business is known to old-timers as "the Peach House" and to others as "Wood's Orchard." Charles was back working the land. He had a connection with the Pleasantville family.

Granny and Grandfather eventually had six children: Rose Custis, Louise, Thomas, James Otho, Paul and Alice. A daughter, Mary, died at age two from diphtheria. Rose was a graduate of Hollins College and Cooper Union art school in New York. She taught school and was the first art supervisor for the Hampton school system. When she married William J. DeReamer, they lived in Crown Point, Indiana, where Uncle De worked at Mapes Consolidated Co. Aunt Rose always planned on coming home to Hampton and had bought property on Chesapeake Avenue and along East Avenue. She also owned the lot on East Avenue and Wythe Place where Mr. Fay Collier had his truck garden. She and Uncle De did return to Hampton in 1951, ready to build their retirement home. At that time, however, a new residential area was being developed on the water down by Armstrong Point. We called that place LaVallett's Meadow and had played there often, sometimes finding arrowheads and even a tomahawk head. Captain LaVallett had raised diamondback turtles for sale to restaurants in Baltimore and New York for turtle soup. He had beached two large barges at the east side of Church Creek for the turtle farm. The storm of 1933 washed over the barges and destroyed his business, but we could still find diamondbacks along the creek after we got home from Petersburg in 1939. Anyway, the new houses were being built on property called "Merrimac Shores." I suppose you could have been standing on that shore to watch the famous Battle of the Ironclads, hence the name. Aunt Rose and Uncle De liked the new area and built one of the first homes there.

Just like the exiled Hamptonians after the Civil War, we all came home: the Matthews family, Uncle Tom, Daisy, Charles and Aunt Rose. Daisy and Charles were my second cousins. I also found that sense of home in the other relatives of that generation—in cousins of the first and second order, removed up or down, and in neighbors around town. We belonged. We knew one another. Everybody knew that summer had arrived when Mr. Victor P. Wilson put on his straw hat. Hampton was that sort of town. We came home because it was home.

There are not very many of us left now who remember those older days, and the younger ones are still getting on with their lives, which is as it should be. But we need to remember that family who grew up on the farm called Pleasantville, and all those others like them who gave us a place in which to live our lives. They kept the land, rebuilt the town and established a community. They accomplished a great many things, and they did not always have the wind at their backs. They rode out several storms besides the one called the Civil War.

Change came inevitably, as it always does. Angelina Massenburg Hickman died in 1885, and Charles Windsor Hickman died in February 1893. The children and their families were all living in town by this time, and the farm would soon pass out of the family and into other hands. No will is found in the city records, but the deed books show that beginning in 1904, parts of the farm were sold by Alice Hickman and the two boys, Charles and Herbert.[379] It seems likely that their father saw the other five girls well settled with responsible husbands and made provisions for Alice, who was unmarried, and his sons. The property was sold piecemeal and changed hands several times. Starting in 1945, R.B. and Elizabeth Thompson began to buy what had been the farm property along Fox Hill and Poor House Roads.[380] In September 1949, they sold a large area for the Hampton Heights Dairy[381] and began to plan for a residential development on the rest of the property. Part of Hampton River was dredged to make a lake, and the whole area was named Elizabeth Lake Estates. Today, many people call it home.

15

Etcetera

For want of a nail, the shoe was lost;
For want of the shoe, the horse was lost;
For want of the horse, the rider was lost;
For want of the rider, the battle was lost;
For want of the battle, the kingdom was lost;
And all for the want of a horseshoe nail.[382]

This old nursery rhyme illustrates the basic idea of cause and effect. From one insignificant thing that did not have to happen came a result that changed the course of the entire nation. Something of the same could be said about Virginia and the Civil War, and although the first cause here was far from insignificant, in my opinion it did not have to happen. The debates during the Secession Convention, whether to remain in the Union or to secede and join the new Confederacy, ultimately hinged on the one proposition that both sides agreed on: there would be no coercion by the Federal government to bring the seceded states back into the Union. The probability that Virginia would change course and adopt secession if force was used was presented to President Lincoln by John Baldwin during their secret meeting on April 4, 1861. Eight days later at Fort Sumter, that "first cause" of war became a reality. The government acted, Virginia seceded, North Carolina followed suit, the Confederacy became viable, a war was fought and the life of the entire nation was changed.

In Virginia, the physical landscape was transformed during the war, but that was eventually restored, renewed or reconstructed. Even those wooden fences that had crisscrossed the state were replaced with the new barbed-wire version. What changed permanently was the size of the state itself. The western fifty counties, known as the Trans-Allegheny region, left the state of Virginia in the spring of 1861, after the adoption of the Secession Resolution. They organized themselves and "rejoined the Union as the new state of West Virginia in 1863."[383]

The societal changes went far deeper. The three Civil War constitutional amendments—the Thirteenth, Fourteenth and Fifteenth—abolished slavery, established the civil rights of all citizens and gave the right of suffrage to black men. The Thirteenth was straightforward: "Neither slavery nor involuntary servitude, except as a punishment for crime whereof the party shall have been duly convicted, shall exist in the United States, or in any place subject to their jurisdiction."[384] The other two amendments were more involved: "The Fourteenth Amendment stipulates that any person born or naturalized in the United States is a citizen, entitled to citizenship rights. Should a state deny the right to vote to any male citizens, its representation in Congress will be proportionally adjusted."[385] Section Three pertained to the citizens of Hampton who had served in the Confederate army and had thus "engaged in insurrection or rebellion against the [Constitution of the United States], or given aid or comfort to the enemies thereof."[386] They had to appear in person at Fort Monroe to take an oath of loyalty to the Union. Section Four of the Fourteenth Amendment removed any hope of restitution for the loss of slave property: "Neither the United States nor any State shall assume or pay…any claim for the loss or emancipation of any slave; but all such debts, obligations and claims shall be held illegal and void."[387]

PASSAGE AND RATIFICATION OF CONSTITUTIONAL AMENDMENTS THIRTEEN, FOURTEEN AND FIFTEEN

Amendment	Passed	Virginia Ratified	Ratified
Thirteenth: Abolition of slavery	January 31, 1865	February 9, 1865	December 6, 1865
Fourteenth: Civil rights	June 13, 1866	October 8, 1869	July 9, 1868
Fifteenth: Black suffrage	February 26, 1869	October 8, 1869	February 2, 1870

The Fifteenth Amendment should have been unambiguous: "The right of citizens of the United States to vote shall not be denied or abridged by the United States or by any State on account of race, color or previous condition of servitude."[388] That was straightforward; black men could vote. The reality at the ballot box was far different. Black men were being systematically disenfranchised. Attitudes of white citizens in both the North and the South were responsible for that disenfranchisement: "The people of the North, with few exceptions, objected as much as did white Southerners to the prospect of social and political equality for blacks."[389] The way to dilute that equality was found by passing state laws that effectively restricted the ability of black men to vote: "The main devices of disfranchisement were the poll tax, registration laws, and literacy and property qualifications, some with the 'understanding clause' or the 'grandfather clause' as loopholes to admit desirable poor whites and illiterates."[390]

In 1902, Virginia identified who could vote by adding new qualifications to the basic ones of being a male citizen at least twenty-one years old. Article II of the new Virginia Constitution in Sections 18, 19, 20, 21, 22 and 38 required the payment of property taxes and poll taxes, and the registration process required being able to read, write and comprehend the language of that legal document. A Confederate veteran, or a son of such a veteran, was excused from paying the poll tax.

In Elizabeth City County and the town of Hampton, black members of the community did not just disappear from the political arena. Many of them eventually moved elsewhere, but those who remained did make a difference: "Scores of descendants of that first generation [of freedmen]—a disproportionate number from so small a town—have made important contributions to their communities and the nation in education, business, and the professions."[391]

At the same time that black men were being denied their right to vote, women in Virginia were organizing for women's suffrage. The movement had essentially begun in the mid-1800s in the North, but the Civil War intervened to delay any progress. Interest picked up when the word "male" was used in the Fourteenth Amendment, and women across the nation prepared for action to acquire their own right to vote. "The first effective...organization in [Virginia] was formed in 1909 and enlisted thousands of Virginia women in the campaign for woman suffrage and related reforms."[392] Women in Hampton had not been politically active, but they realized that they would make a difference if they could vote on issues relating to their families. After taking that position, they accepted the responsibility for looking out for the interests of other women's households. They organized: "Their action marked a departure from the Virginia tradition of the 'moral influence' of women in regard to social and political issues."[393]

Change had come across the South, and "the fair little town of Hampton" was no longer the peaceful backwater across Hampton Roads from the bustling city of Norfolk. In 1910, historian Lyon G. Tyler wrote:

> *In the forty-five years since the war, the population of Elizabeth City County is upwards of 26,000 and that of Hampton very near 8,000. The town has handsome paved streets and sidewalks, electric lights, electric cars* [streetcars], *fine stores and bank buildings, and is connected with Richmond by one of the best railroad lines in the Union, while the wharf at Old Point is the stopping place of steamers to Norfolk, to Washington, and to Baltimore and New York. Indeed, the whole region of what was known, in 1619, as "Elizabeth City Corporation," has greatly improved…and its appearance is a monument to the industry of its inhabitants.*[394]

Cause and effect had brought war and destruction to Virginia. The hard work and determination of the citizens of Elizabeth City County and Hampton had brought rebirth out of that wartime desolation. The county and the town were moving into the twentieth century with the full knowledge of who they were.

Appendix

Charles Winsor Hickman/ Angelina Massenburg Hickman Family

In order to provide the "who's who" information for the text, the following listing of my grandmother's family is provided. Four generations are included, starting with Granny's parents, Charles Windsor Hickman and Angelina Massenburg Hickman. The second generation lists Granny (Angelina) and her seven siblings, with their children as the third generation. The fourth-generation members listed are Granny's grandchildren, including my brothers and sisters, and my second cousins, who are mentioned in the body of the text. The third-generation family members who died as infants or young children are indicated with an (*). I hope this helps with identification. We were a large family.

First	**Second**
Charles Winsor Hickman 1815–1893 /m. Angelina Massenburg Hickman 1827–1885	
	Mary Winsor Hickman 1848–/m. Charles Phillips 1838–
	Alice Hickman 1850–1943
	Charles Winsor Hickman Jr. 1852–1912 /m. Phoebe Estes 1856–1927
	Martha "Mattie" Hickman 1855–1896 /m1 Henry Lane Schmelz 1853–1914 /m2 Annie Moomaw
	Georgia "Georgie" Hickman 1857–1909 /m. George Anton Schmelz 1855–1911

Third	Fourth
Arthur	
Grace /m. John Garland Pollard	
Louis	
Carroll	
Garland	
Charles	
Susan	
Georgia	
Mamie	
Elliott E.	
Charlton L.	
Frank W.	
Corneille Hickman /m. John Wood	
	Charles Wood
Mattie*	
Ethel	
Susan Lelia*	
Dorothy	
Catherine Curle	
Margaret	
Angeline	
Ruth	
Hilda Schmelz /m. William R. Van Buren	
	William R. Van Buren Jr.
Elsie	
F. Anton*	
Myrtle*	
Frank H.*	
George Anton Jr.*	
Nancy Belle*	

First	Second
	Angelina Hickman "Granny" 1859–1953 /m. Thomas Hanson Parramore 1850–1912
	Lelia Hickman 1864–1896 /m. James Mc Menamin 1847–1901
	Herbert Hickman 1866–1935 /m1. Mildred Warren; m2. Lula Abrams

THIRD	FOURTH
Rose Custis /m. William J. de Reamer	
Mary*	
Louise	
Thomas H. /m. Jesse Black	
	Thomas
James Otho /m. Grace Ryan	
	James
	Mary
Paul Jones /m. Jane Oliver	
	Paul Jones Jr.
	John
Alice Hickman /m. Joseph James Matthews	
	Joseph James "Jimmy"
	Mary Louise
	William Parramore
	Angeline
	Alice Rose
Charles*	
Mary	
James	
John /m. Dorothy Bullard	
	Ann
	Marguerite "Daisy"
	Dorothy "Lollie"
Lelia Elizabeth*	
Mildred	
Warren	
Howard	
George	
Earl	

Notes

Chapter 1

1. Tyler, *History*, 15.
2. Horn, *Land*, 256.
3. Tyler, *History*, 16, 18.
4. Ibid., 28.
5. Ibid., 29.
6. Ibid., 14.
7. Bentley, *Gravestone Inscriptions*, 1.
8. Tyler, *History*, 50.
9. Ibid., 51.
10. Adapted from Lyon G. Tyler, *History of Hampton and Elizabeth City County* (Virginia, 1922), 50.
11. E.A. Semple map.
12. Appendix: Charles Windsor Hickman/Angelina Massenburg Hickman Family.
13. Index to Deeds.
14. Elliott, *Fox Hill*, 8.
15. Ibid.
16. Ibid., 47, 52.
17. Ibid., 52.
18. Ibid., 25–26.
19. Tyler, *History*, 51.
20. Ibid., 46.

21. Betts, *Visitors' Hand Book*, 18–20.
22. Quarstein and Mroczkowski, *Fort Monroe*, 23.
23. Betts, *Visitors' Hand Book*, 11–12.

CHAPTER 2

24. Cassidy, "Among the Old Words," 295–97.

CHAPTER 3

25. Elliott, *Fox Hill*, 21–22.
26. Tyler, *History*, 21.
27. Ibid., 22.
28. Ibid., 48.
29. Elliott, *Fox Hill*, 21–22.
30. E.A. Semple map
31. Tyler, *History*, 54.

CHAPTER 4

32. Tyler, *History*, 38.
33. James, *Disappearance*, 11.
34. Ibid., 8.
35. Ibid.
36. Tormey, *How Firm*, 54.
37. James, *Disappearance*, 12.
38. Hoffer, *Counties*, 74.
39. Acts of the General Assembly, 28, 32..
40. U.S. census, 1850.
41. U.S. census, 1860.
42. U.S. census, 1870.
43. Ailor and Hawkins, *Little England Chapel*, 14.
44. Ibid., 15.
45. Ibid., 23, 27, 29.
46. Department of Commerce and Labor, *Paupers*.
47. Transcribed and adapted from the original hand-written archival document at Library of Virginia. Auditor of Public Accounts, Entry 739, Reports of the Overseers of the Poor, 1851, Elizabeth City, Courtesy of Library of Virginia, Richmond.

CHAPTER 5

48. Freehling and Simpson, *Showdown*, ix.
49. Craven, *Coming*, 149.
50. Ibid., 174.
51. Freehling and Simpson, *Showdown*, xi.
52. Ibid.
53. Freehling and Simpson, *Showdown*, xi.
54. Ibid., 24, footnote.
55. Ibid., xv.
56. Ibid., 42.
57. Reese, *Proceedings*, 1:49.
58. Ibid., 1:129.
59. Gaines, *Biographical Register*, 14.
60. Freehling and Simpson, *Showdown*, 80.
61. Ibid., 78–79.
62. Freehling and Simpson, *Showdown*, 56.
63. Ibid., 103.
64. Ibid., 72–73.
65. Freehling and Simpson, *Showdown*, 92–93.
66. Reese, *Proceedings*, 1:III, IV.
67. Ibid., 3:163–64.
68. Gaines, *Biographical Register*, 55.
69. Reese, *Proceedings*, 1:410.
70. Ibid.
71. Elliott, *Fox Hill*, 28.
72. Freehling and Simpson, *Showdown*, 131.
73. Ibid., 154.
74. Nelson and Sheriff, *People at War*, 53
75. Magruder, "Piece of Secret History," 438–45.
76. Hall, "Lincoln's Intcrvicw," 262.
77. Reese, *Proceedings*, 3:650.
78. Ibid., 3:724–728.
79. Freehling and Simpson, *Showdown*, 181.
80. Ibid., 183.
81. Reese, *Proceedings*, 3:735.
82. Ibid., 3:730.
83. Ibid., 4:26.
84. Ibid., 4:76.
85. Ibid., 4:124.
86. Ibid., 4:127.
87. Ibid., 4:25.

88. Ibid., 4:144.
89. Ibid., 4:146.
90. Ibid., 4:126.

Chapter 6

91. Quarstein, *Civil War*, 18.
92. Ibid.
93. Ibid., 19.
94. Engs, *Freedom's First Generation*, 17–18.
95. Quarstein, *Civil War*, 22.
96. Ibid., 23.
97. Molineux, *Young Virginia Boatman*, 13, note 7.
98. Quarstein and Mroczkowski, *Fort Monroe*, 67–70.
99. Engs, *Freedom's First Generation*, 18.
100. Ibid., 20.
101. Molineux, *Young Virginia Boatman*, 13.
102. Ibid., 77.
103. Ibid., 34–35.
104. Ibid., 37.
105. Ibid., 37.
106. Quarstein and Clevenger, *Old Point Comfort Resort*, 36.
107. Molineaux, *Young Virginia Boatman*, 29.
108. Daly, *Naval Letters*, 234.
109. Alexander, *African American History*, 34.
110. Elliott, *Fox Hill*, 40.
111. Molineux, *Young Virginia Boatman*, 7, 9, 11, 38–39.
112. Military Map of the Peninsula, Plate 18.
113. Elliott, *Fox Hill*, 44–45.
114. Sauers, *Succession*, 152.
115. Cobb, "Rehearsing Reconstruction in Occupied Virginia," 151.
116. Sauers, *Succession*, 18, 96.
117. Ibid., 119.
118. Ibid., 120.
119. Quarstein, *Civil War*, 63.
120. Quarstein and Mroczkowski, *Fort Monroe*, 124.
121. Quarstein, *Civil War*, 45.
122. Charles, *Hampton Ink*, 157.
123. Ibid.
124. Quarstein, *Civil War*, 91.
125. Haydon, *Aeronautics*, 85–86.

126. Ibid., 87.
127. Ibid., 88.
128. Evans, *War of the Aeronauts*, 21–22.
129. Ibid., 23.
130. Haydon, *Aeronautics*, 92.
131. Ibid.
132. Haydon, *Aeronautics*, 93
133. Ibid., 94.
134. Ibid., 96.
135. Ibid., 101.
136. Ibid., 103.
137. Ibid., 112.
138. Ibid., 345.
139. Ibid., 373.
140. Evans, *War of the Aeronauts*, 174.
141. Ibid., 189.
142. Ibid., 194.
143. Ibid., 196.
144. Ibid.
145. Ibid.
146. Ibid., 199.
147. Ibid., 244.

CHAPTER 7

148. Dew, *Review*, 6.
149. Greenberg, *Confessions*, 3.
150. Turner, *Confessions*.
151. Greenberg, *Confessions*, 8.
152. Polk, "Analysis," 50.
153. Ibid., 65.
154. Ibid., 266–67.
155. Ibid., 268.
156. Ibid., 72.
157. Dew, *Review*, 5.
158. Ibid., 47.
159. Polk, "Analysis," 33.
160. Ibid., 78.
161. Ibid., 80.
162. Ibid.
163. Ibid., 86.

164. Ibid., 85.
165. Ibid., 80.
166. Morison, *Oxford History*, 435.
167. Engs, *Freedom's First Generation*, 67.
168. Alexander, *African American History*, 47.
169. Ibid., 40–41.
170. Engs, *Freedom's First Generation*, 30.
171. Ibid., 31.
172. Ibid., 33.
173. Nelson and Sheriff, *People at War*, 80.
174. Engs, *Freedom's First Generation*, XVII.
175. Ibid., 14.
176. Ibid., 67.

CHAPTER 8

177. Nelson and Sheriff, *People at War*, 264.
178. Ibid., 95.

CHAPTER 9

179. Nelson and Sheriff, *People at War*, 285.
180. Engs, *Freedom's First Generation*, 34; Alexander, *African American History*, 84.
181. Engs, *Freedom's First Generation*, 180.
182. Ibid., 174.
183. Blum, *National Experience*, 390.
184. Quoted in Engs, *Freedom's First Generation*, 161.
185. Molineux, *Young Virginia Boatman*, 125.
186. Ibid., 127.
187. Ibid., 125.
188. Ibid.
189. *(Baltimore, MD) Sun*, quoted in Charles, *Hampton Ink*, 210.
190. Evans, *Lost Landmarks*, 44.
191. Ibid.
192. Fire Alarm Signal Map.
193. Evans, *Lost Landmarks*, 57.
194. Brown, *Newport News*, 103.
195. Fort Monroe, *Tales of Old Fort Monroe*, Number 10.
196. Quarstein and Clevenger, *Old Point Comfort Resort*, 40.
197. Molineux, *Young Virginia Boatman*, 115.
198. Nelson and Sheriff, *People at War*, 264.

199. Index to Deeds, Book 2, 369; Book 4, 386; Book 6, 87, 89, 420; Book 15, 10,13; Book 16, 362; Book 25, 380.
200. Evans, *Lost Landmarks*, 14.
201. Elliott, *Fox Hill*, 73.
202. Index to Deeds, Book 36, 473.
203. Ibid., Book 25, 456; Book 31, 151; Book 32, 492.
204. Ibid, Book 45, 247; Book 45, 250; Book 46, 505.
205. Molineux, *Young Virginia Boatman*, 126.
206. Engs, *Freedom's First Generation*, 164
207. Cudahy, *Short History*.
208. Rouse, *Streetcars*.
209. Evans, *Lost Landmarks*, 15.
210. Elliott, *Fox Hill*, 73.
211. Ibid., 59.
212. Rouse, "Streetcars."
213. Betts, *Visitors' Hand Book*, 82.
214. Ibid., 84.
215. Elliott, *Fox Hill*, 66.
216. Ibid., 22.
217. Chowning, *Harvesting*, 147.
218. David Niebuhr, executive director, Waterman's Museum, interview with the author, Yorktown, Virginia.
219. Chowning, *Harvesting*, 154–55.
220. Ibid., 150.
221. Ibid., 153.
222. Niebuhr, interview with the author.
223. Chowning, *Harvesting*, p. 153
224. Ibid.
225. Ibid., 156.
226. Ibid., 147.
227. Elliott, *Fox Hill*, 47–48.
228. Ibid.
229. Molineux, *Young Virginia Boatman*, 127.
230. Tyler, *History*, 54.
231. Ibid., 52.
232. Cobb, *Optic Views*.
233. Betts, *Visitors' Hand Book*, 24–26.
234. Ibid., 26.
235. Ibid., 29.
236. Ibid., 31.
237. Molineux, *Young Virginia Boatman*, 129.

CHAPTER 10

238. Elliott, *Fox Hill*, 79.
239. Industry Number of *Hampton Monitor*, August 1907, bound copy, advertisement on the last page.
240. Cobb, Holt, Smith, Hicks and Hampton History Museum, *Hampton*, 53.
241. Newcombe, *Biology*, 13.
242. Cobb, Holt, Smith, Hicks and Hampton History Museum, *Hampton*, 59.
243. Chowning, *Harvesting*, 197.
244. Ibid., 252–53.
245. Newcombe, *Biology*, 13.
246. Ibid., 9.
247. Byrd, *Oyster*, 4.
248. Ibid., 7.
249. Rouse, "Streetcars," 55.
250. Ibid.
251. Corson, *Oyster Industry*, 39.
252. Ibid.
253. Ibid., 9.
254. Ibid., 10.
255. Ibid., 37.
256. Ibid., 12.
257. Ibid., 13.
258. Ibid.
259. Ibid., 14.
260. Ibid., 21.
261. Ibid., 22.
262. Ibid.
263. Elliott, *Fox Hill*, 60.
264. McMurry and Fay, *Chemistry*, 582, 586.
265. Evans, *Lost Landmarks*, 17.

CHAPTER 11

266. Engs, *Freedom's First Generation*, 75.
267. Ibid., 29.
268. Goodall, *American Slave Code*, 320–321.
269. Ibid., 321.
270. Engs, *Freedom's First Generation*, 12.
271. Ibid., 47.
272. Ibid., 13.
273. Ibid., 54.

274. Ibid., 48.
275. Ibid., 50.
276. Ibid., 54.
277. Ibid., 64.
278. Tyler, *History*, 53.
279. First Annual Report, 5.
280. Ibid., 15.
281. Ibid., 12.
282. Ibid., 5.
283. Ibid., 15.
284. Ibid., 193.
285. Ibid., 177, 188, 192, 201.
286. Seventh Annual Report, 9.
287. Ibid., 34.
288. Ibid., 3.
289. Engs, *Freedom's First Generation*, 67.
290. Ibid., 70.
291. Ibid., 61.
292. Ibid., 175–76.
293. Ibid., 74–75.
294. Ibid., 72.
295. Ibid., 85.
296. Ibid., 90.
297. Ailor and Hawkins, *Little England Chapel*, 5.
298. Ibid., 10.
299. Ibid.
300. Ibid., 13.
301. Ibid., 17.
302. Engs, *Freedom's First Generation*, 180.
303. Ibid., 174.
304. Ibid.
305. Ibid., 168–69.
306. Ibid., 76.
307. Ibid., 79.
308. Engs, *Educating*, 73.
309. Ibid.
310. Ibid., xiii.
311. Ibid., 73.
312. Ibid., xix.
313. Ibid.
314. Betts, *Visitors' Guide Book*, 36–37.
315. Engs, *Freedom's First Generation*, 148.

316. Betts, *Visitors' Guide Book*, 38.
317. Engs, *Educating*, 102.
318. Ibid., 80.
319. Ibid., 79.
320. Ibid., 134.
321. Ibid., 101.
322. Ibid., 102–03.
323. Ibid., 103.
324. Betts, *Visitors' Guide Book*, 42–43.
325. Ibid., 44.
326. Engs, *Freedom's First Generation*, 159–60.
327. Engs, *Educating*, 106.
328. Ibid., 110–11.
329. Ibid.
330. Ibid.
331. Betts, *Visitors' Guide Book*, 47.
332. Engs, *Educating*, 117.
333. Ibid.
334. Betts, *Visitors' Guide Book*, 38–39.
335. Engs, *Educating*, 119.
336. Ibid., 121, 123.
337. Ibid., 121.
338. Ibid., 122.
339. Engs, *Educating*, 122.
340. Ibid.
341. Ibid., 132.
342. Ibid., 128.
343. Ibid., 106.
344. Ibid., 107.
345. Engs, *Freedom's First Generation*, 159.

Chapter 12

346. Randy Cabell, notation
347. "Bonnie Blue Flag," http://civilwar.bluegrass.net/FlagsUniformsAndInsignia/bonnieblueflag.html.
348. Lake, *History*.
349. Ailor and Hawkins, *Little England Chapel*, 15.
350. Ibid., 23.
351. Engs, *Educating*, 87.

352. *Sentara Hampton General Hospital*, 7.
353. Ibid.
354. Ibid., 18.
355. Quarstein and Clervenger, *Old Point Comfort Resort*, 47.
356. Ibid., 48.
357. Ibid., 47.

CHAPTER 13

358. Industrial Number, 4.
359. Ibid., 10.
360. Ibid., 12.
361. Ibid., 5.
362. Ibid.
363. Industrial Number, 5.
364. Ibid.
365. Ibid., 5–6.
366. Ibid., 19.
367. Ibid.
368. *Daily Press*, Sunday, January 13, 1907, 6.
369. Quarstein and Clevenger, *Old Point Comfort Resort*, 54.
370. Ibid., 64.
371. *Daily Press*, March 9, 1907, 6.
372. Ibid., March 21, 1907, 1.
373. Ibid., April 16, 1907, 1.
374. Ibid., April 18, 1907, 6.
375. Ibid., April 19, 1907, 6; March 1,1907, 7.
376. Ibid., April 26, 1907, 1.
377. Yarsimske, *Jamestown Exposition*, 105.
378. Ibid., 103.

CHAPTER 14

379. Index of Deeds, Book RD$_4$, 378.
380. Ibid., Book 129, 421; Book 134, 378; Book 141, 65; Book 159, 6; Book 165, 306; Book 179, 13; Book 187, 210.
381. Ibid, Book 188, 386.

CHAPTER 15

382. Old English proverb.
383. Nelson and Sheriff, *People at War*, 69.
384. U.S. Constitution.
385. Nelson and Sheriff, *People at War*, 341.
386. U.S. Constitution.
387. Ibid.
388. Ibid.
389. Blum, *National Experience*, 408.
390. Ibid., 418–19.
391. Engs, *Freedom's First Generation*, 204.
392. Erickson, "Women's Rights," vi.
393. Ibid., 2.
394. Tyler, *History*, 55–56.

Bibliography

Acts of the General Assembly of Virginia passed in 1857–58. Richmond, VA: William F. Ritche, Public Printer of the General Assembly of Virginia.

Ailor, Osceola Savage, and Carolyn Halderman Hawkins. *Little England Chapel: A Black Landmark in Hampton, Virginia*. Hampton, VA: Gear-Up Printing, 1993.

Alexander, Cassandra L. Newby. *An African American History of the Civil War in Hampton Roads*. Charleston, SC: The History Press, 2010.

Bentley, John B. *Gravestone Inscriptions from the Cemetery of St. John's Episcopal Church, Hampton, Virginia*. Published for St. John's Church by the Hugh S. Watson Jr. Genealogical Society of Tidewater Virginia, Thomas Nelson Community College, Hampton, Virginia.

Betts, C.W. *Visitors' Hand Book of Old Point Comfort, Va., and Vicinity*. 3rd ed. Hampton, VA: Press of the Hampton Institute, 1885.

Blum, John M., et al. *The National Experience: A History of the United States*. New York: Harcourt Brace Jovanovich, Inc., 1981.

"Bonnie Blue Flag." http://civilwar.bluegrass.net/FlagsUniformsAndInsignia/bonnieblueflag.html.

Brown, Alexander Crosby, ed. *Newport News Anniversary Edition, 325 Years*. Newport News, VA: Newport News Golden Anniversary Corporation, 1946.

Byrd, Governor Harry F. *The Oyster Industry and County Government*. Governor to the General Assembly of Virginia, Tuesday, January 31, 1928. House Document No. 8. Richmond, VA: Davis Bottom, Superintendent of Public Printing, 1928.

Cassidy, Frederick G. "Among the Old Words." *American Speech* 55, no. 4 (Winter 1980).

Charles, Joan D. *Hampton Ink, 1707 to 1932*. Hampton, VA, 2009.
Chowning, Larry S. *Harvesting the Chesapeake: Tools and Traditions*. Centreville, MD: Tidewater Publishers, 1990.
Cobb, E.L. *Optic Views and Impressions of the National Soldiers' Home, South Branch N.H.D.V.S., near Hampton, Virginia*. South Branch, VA: NHDVS, 1910.
Cobb, J. Michael. "Rehearsing Reconstruction in Occupied Virginia: Life and Emancipation at Fort Monroe." In *Virginia at War, 1864*. Edited by William C. Davis and James I. Robertson Jr. Lexington: University of Kentucky Press, 2009.
Cobb, J. Michael, Wythe Holt, Tim Smith, Ed Hicks and the Hampton History Museum. *Hampton*. Charleston, SC: Arcadia Publishing, 2008.
Corson, J.J., III. *The Oyster Industry of Virginia: Being a Series of Articles Appearing in the Richmond News Leader, January 9–16, 1930*. Pamphlet. Virginia State Library, Richmond, 1930.
Craven, Avery. *The Coming of the Civil War*. 2nd ed. Chicago: University of Chicago Press, 1957.
Cudahy, Brian J. *A Short History Mass Transportation in America*. Washington, D.C.: American Public Tansit Association, 1983.
Daly, Robert W., ed. *Naval Letters Series*. Vol. 1, *Aboard the USS* Monitor*: 1862, The Letters of Acting Paymaster William Frederick Keeler, U.S. Navy to His Wife, Anna*. Annapolis, MD: Naval Institute, 1964.
Department of Commerce and Labor, Bureau of the Census. *Paupers in Almshouses 1904*. Special Report. Washington, D.C.: Government Printing Office, 1906.
Dew, Thomas R. *Review of the Debate in the Virginia Legislature of 1831 and 1832*. Richmond, VA: Printed by T.W. White, 1832.
Elliott, Charles F. *Fox Hill, Its People and Places: A History of Fox Hill, Virginia*. N.p.: privately printed, 1976.
Engs, Robert Francis. *Educating the Disfranchised and the Disinherited: Samuel Chapman Armstrong and Hampton Institute, 1839–1893*. Knoxville: University of Tennessee Press, 1999.
———. *Freedom's First Generation: Black Hampton, Virginia, 1861–1890*. Philadelphia: University of Pennsylvania Press, 1979.
Erickson, Alice Matthews. "Women's Rights in Virginia, 1909–1920." Master's thesis, College of William and Mary, Williamsburg, VA, 1975.
Evans, Charles M. *The War of the Aeronauts: A History of Ballooning During the Civil War*. Mechanicsburg, PA: Stackpole Books, 2002.
Evans, Hamilton H. *Lost Landmarks of Old Hampton, Revolutionary War Port Town*. Hampton, VA: Hampton Association for the Arts and Humanities, 1976.
Fire Alarm Signal Map, Hampton, 1907.
First Annual Report of the Superintendent of Public Instruction for the Year Ending August 31, 1871. Richmond, VA: C.A. Schaffter, Superintendent Public Printing, 1871.

Fort Monroe Casemate Museum. *Tales of Old Fort Monroe*. Hampton, VA: Fort Monroe, 1962.

Freehling, William W., and Craig M. Simpson, eds. *Showdown in Virginia: The 1861 Convention and the Fate of the Union*. Charlottesville: University of Virginia Press, 2010.

Gaines, William H., Jr. *Biographical Register of Members of the Virginia State Convention of 1861, First Session*. Virginia State Library, Richmond, 1969.

Goodall, William. *The American Slave Code: In Theory and Practice*. New York: American and Foreign Anti-Slavery Society, 1853.

Greenberg, Kenneth S., ed. *The Confessions of Nat Turner and Related Documents*. Boston, MA: St. Martin's Press, Bedford Books, 1996.

Hall, Wilmer L. "Lincoln's Interview with John B. Baldwin." *South Atlantic Quarterly* (July 1914).

Haydon, F. Stansbury. *Aeronautics in the Union and Confederate Armies, with a Survey of Military Aeronautics Prior to 1861*. Baltimore, MD: Johns Hopkins Press, 1941.

The History: Compassionate Caring at Sentara Hampton General Hospital, 1892–1992. Pamphlet, 1992.

Hoffer, Frank William. *Counties in Transition: A Study of County Public and Private Welfare Administration in Virginia*. Charlottesville: Institute for Research in the Social Services, University of Virginia, 1929.

Horn, James. *A Land as God Made It: Jamestown and the Birth of America*. New York: Basic Books, 2005.

Index to Deeds, Trusts, etc. Deed Book Room. Hampton, Virginia Courthouse.

James, Arthur W. *The Disappearance of the County Almshouse in Virginia: Back from "Over the Hill."* Richmon, VA: State Board of Public Welfare, 1926.

Lake, Jeffrey L. *History of Public Health in Virginia*. Richmond: Virginia Department of Health, 2004.

Magruder, Allan B. "A Piece of Secret History." *Atlantic Monthly* (April 1875).

McHugh, J.L. *Status of the Blue Crab Fishery in Chesapeake Bay*. Gloucester Point: Virginia Fisheries Laboratory, 1957.

McMurry, John, and Robert C. Fay. *Chemistry*. Englewood Cliffs, NJ: Prentice Hall, 1995.

Military Map of the Peninsula Department. Major General J.A. Dix, commander Seventh Army Corps. Plate 18, April 1862, Campaign Maps, Army of the Potomac, Yorktown to Williamsburg. From *The Official Military Atlas of the Civil War*. New York: Fairfax Press, 1983.

Molineux, Will, ed. *A Young Virginia Boatman Navigates the Civil War: The Journals of George Randolph Wood*. Charlottesville: University of Virginia Press, 2010.

Morison, Samuel Eliot, *The Oxford History of the American People*. Vol. 2, *1789 Through Reconstruction*. New York: Oxford University Press, 1972.

Nelson, Scott Reynolds, and Carol Sheriff. *A People at War: Civilians and Soldiers in America's Civil War*. New York: Oxford University Press, 2007.

Newcombe, Curtis L. *The Biology and Conservation of the Blue Crab*. Richmond, VA: Division of Purchase and Print, 1943

Olde Wythe Neighborhood Association. *Hampton's Olde Wythe*. Charleston, SC: Arcadia Publishing, 2006.

Polk, Lee Rivers. "An Analysis of Argumentation in the Virginia Slavery Debate of 1832." Thesis, Purdue University, 1967.

Quarstein, John V. *The Civil War on the Virginia Peninsula*. Charleston, SC: Arcadia Publishing, 1997.

Quarstein, John V., and Dennis Mroczkowski. *Fort Monroe: The Key to the South*. Charleston, SC: Arcadia Publishing, 2000.

Quarstein, John V., and Julie Steere Clevenger. *Old Point Comfort Resort: Hospitality, Health and History on Virginia's Chesapeake Bay*. Charleston, SC: The History Press, 2009.

Reese, George H., ed. *Proceedings of the Virginia State Convention of 1861, February 13–May 1, In Four Volumes*. Virginia State Library, Richmond, 1965.

Rouse, Parke. "Streetcars Traversed Peninsula before WWII." *Daily Press*, April 4, 1993.

Sauers, Richard A. *A Succession of Honorable Victories: The Burnside Expedition in North Carolina*. Dayton, OH: Morningside House, Inc., 1996.

Seventh Annual Report of the Superintendent of Public Instruction for the year ending July 31, 1877, Richmond, VA: R.F. Walker, Superintendent of Public Instruction, 1877.

Tormey, James. *How Firm a Foundation*. Richmond, VA: Dietz Press, 2009.

Turner, Nat. *Confessions*. Richmond, VA: Thomas R. Gray, 1832.

Tyler, Lyon G. *History of Hampton and Elizabeth City County, Virginia*. Hampton, VA: Board of Supervisors of Elizabeth City County, 1922.

United States Census Records. United States Government. Washington, D.C.

Yarsinske, Amy Waters. *Jamestown Exposition: American Imperialism on Parade*. Vols. 1–2. Charleston, SC: Arcadia Publishing, 1999.

Newspapers

Daily Press, Newport News, Virginia

Hampton Bulletin, National Soldiers' Home

Hampton Monitor, Hampton, Virginia

Sun, Baltimore, Maryland

Index

H

J

K

L

M

O

P

R

S

About the Author

The author in a large live oak tree planted by her great-grandfather on what used to be the Pleasantville farm. The area is now called the Elizabeth Lakes residential area of Hampton. *Photograph taken by Nancy Forbes.*

Alice Matthews Erickson is a ninth-generation Virginian. She received an AB degree in English from the College of William and Mary. She was the 1957–58 Exeter Scholar from William and Mary to the University of Exeter, England, where she carried out graduate studies in English literature. She also earned an MA degree in history from the College of William and Mary. She has taught courses in both English and history at high school and college levels. Her interest in the Civil War comes from her family's experience under Federal occupation in the war years, 1861–1865. This book was inspired by the desire to write down the family stories before they are lost to memory and to explore the history of civilian life in Hampton and Elizabeth City County shortly before, during and after the war. Alice and her husband, Wayne, live in Williamsburg, Virginia. They have one son, John, who lives with his family in Pennsylvania.

Visit us at
www.historypress.net